Know Your Ohio Government

The definitive guide for citizens who want to learn how to influence government policies.

The League of Women Voters of Ohio Education Fund
Ninth Edition 2004

The League of Women Voters of Ohio Education Fund is indebted to the many individuals in state government who generously provided information for this revision.

Research and revision by Scott Shelton
Editing by Chris Moran
Cover graphics by Bonnie App
Layout by Scott Britton
Additional editing by Bonnie App, Scott Britton, Terry McCoy, and Peg Rosenfield

Copies may be ordered from
THE LEAGUE OF WOMEN VOTERS OF OHIO EDUCATION FUND
17 South High Street, Suite 650
Columbus, Ohio 43215
(614) 469-1505
www.lwvohio.org
sales@lwvohio.org

 The League of Women Voters of Ohio Education Fund, a nonpartisan political organization, encourages the informed and active participation of citizens in government and works to increase understanding of major public policy issues.

Introduction

The League of Women Voters of Ohio Education Fund first published *Know Your Ohio Government* in 1964 as a guide to the state's system of political organization and policy making. Each edition since has incorporated the many changes that have taken place in the laws and governance of the state of Ohio. This edition includes recent changes in state government, including homeland security updates, resolution of the *DeRolph* decision, and information regarding the 2002 Help America Vote Act (HAVA) and its implications for voters.

This publication is offered to the citizens of Ohio as a resource for understanding and participating in state government. The strength and effectiveness of our democratic form of government depend on the informed and active participation of citizens in government and the political process.

The League of Women Voters of Ohio Education Fund is a nonpartisan educational organization that seeks to increase public understanding of major public policy issues and to promote awareness of the options available in government decision making. The League also provides educational services, research, publications, and conferences to enable citizens to take part more effectively in the democratic process.

Contents

CHAPTER ONE

This is Ohio

O hio, nicknamed "the Buckeye State," was admitted to the union on March 1, 1803, as the 17th state. It shares its northern boundary with Michigan and with Canada through the middle of Lake Erie, its eastern boundary with Pennsylvania and West Virginia, its southern boundary with West Virginia and Kentucky, and its western boundary with Indiana.

Ohio is 34th in area among the 50 states, with a land area of 44,828 square miles. According to 2002 U.S. Census Bureau estimates, Ohio's population is 11,421,267, placing it seventh in rank, following California, Texas, New York, Florida, Illinois, and Pennsylvania. Ohio's central location puts it within a 600-mile radius of 60 percent of the U.S. population. In addition, 50 percent of Canada's population is within the same 600-mile radius of Ohio.

The temperate climate and adequate rainfall provide a climate suitable for growing a wide range of agricultural products. Lake Erie, the Ohio River, and the numerous other inland lakes and rivers provide an abundant water supply.

Until the industrial revolution of the late 1800s Ohio was primarily an agrarian society, in part because of varying soils and conditions and in part because of the diverse backgrounds of its settlers. With its central location and easy access to waterways and to natural resources, grew into an important manufacturing and distribution center. The Industrial Revolution played a major role in Ohio's development, and Ohio continues to have a large manufacturing base. The major industries of the state include manufacturing (machinery, transportation equipment, fabricated metal, rubber and plastic products, food products, and chemicals), service industries and financial services. In recent years Ohio's economy has become more service oriented and is playing a major role in emerging technologies such as biotechnology. Ohio has the seventh largest

State Flower

The red carnation was adopted in 1904 as a posthumous tribute to President William McKinley, who was born in Niles, Ohio. The red carnation had been McKinley's favorite lapel decoration.

economy in the United States and the third largest manufacturing sector in the nation. Ohio has one of the most diversified economies, too, ranking third behind Missouri and Pennsylvania.

Ohio's largest cities (2002 Census Bureau estimates) are Columbus, 725,228; Cleveland, 467,851; and Cincinnati, 323,885. Toledo, Akron, Dayton, Youngstown, and Canton are also major cities.

Ohio's History

The area that makes up Ohio has a rich history that predates statehood. Archaeological studies show that prehistoric Native Americans, notably the Hopewell and Adena, migrated to the Ohio area approximately 5,000 years ago. These Native Americans built more than a thousand mounds around the state; the most famous is the Serpent Mound in southwestern Ohio. There are reminders of some of the other early Native American in the names of counties, towns, and rivers such as Miami, Wyandot, Ottawa, Delaware, Cuyahoga, Seneca, Tuscaroras (Tuscarawas), and Shawnee, and in the name of the great lake, Erie.

State Economy

According to the Ohio Department of Development, if Ohio were its own nation it would have the 20th largest economy in the world.

With Lake Erie on the north and the Ohio River on the east and south both offering access to Ohio by water, explorers, hunters, and trappers knew the territory long before there was any effort at settlement. Early settlement attempts ended in failure; fighting between frontiersmen and the Delaware Indians, as well as the effects of the Revolutionary War on the frontier, de-

State Flag

Architect John Eisemann designed Ohio's flag in 1901. The Ohio flag is the only pennant-shaped state flag in the United States. The swallow-tailed shape symbolizes Ohio's hills and valleys; the red and white stripes represent roadways and waterways; the initial "O" and the buckeye are represented by the white circle with its red center; the stars grouped around the circle represent the original 13 states of the Union; and the four extra stars represent Ohio's status as the 17th state.

Statehood . . . 150 Years Later

On August 7, 1953, Ohio was formally admitted to the Union by a joint resolution of Congress. Just as Ohio prepared to celebrate its 150th anniversary in 1953, researchers discovered that a joint session of Congress had never declared Ohio a state. No state before Ohio had been formally admitted through a joint resolution, as the practice began in 1812. Therefore, in 1953, Congress formally declared Ohio a state— retroactive to 1803. President Eisenhower signed the joint resolution on August 7.

(Cincinnati Enquirer, *February 19, 2003)*

layed further undertakings for quite some time. Even after the signing of the Treaty of Paris in 1783 ended the Revolutionary War, it was not until 1788 that the first permanent settlement was established at Marietta.

Under the Articles of Confederation, the U.S. Congress in 1784 enacted an ordinance for governing the western lands ceded by New York, Virginia, Massachusetts, and Connecticut. It was superseded by the Northwest Ordinance of 1787 and was the basis for the formation of six states, including Ohio. The U.S. Congress appointed a governor, a secretary, and three judges to govern the new territory.

The Northwest Ordinance stated that, when there existed "5,000 free male inhabitants of full age," the settlers were allowed to elect a General Assembly, or legislative body, for the territory. The first General Assembly met in Cincinnati in 1799 and consisted of the governor, the Legislative Council, and the House of Representatives.

Representatives had to be men and "be possessed of 200 acres of land." The U.S. Congress selected the five members of the Legislative Council from ten nominees submitted by the U.S. House of Representatives. The Legislative Council members were required to own 500 acres of land. All Ohio public officials had to fulfill certain residency requirements as well. William Tiffin was elected the first speaker of the House, and William Henry Harrison was elected as the territory's representative to Congress.

The second General Assembly met in Chillicothe from November 1801 to January 1802, and on April 30, 1802, Congress authorized the formation of a government for Ohio. That November the first Constitutional Convention convened in Chillicothe. With Edward Tiffin as president, the delegates drafted and adopted Ohio's first Constitution.

The first election for governor, General Assembly, and officials of the nine newly created counties was held in January 1803. Edward Tiffin became the first governor of Ohio.

The capital was located in Chillicothe until 1810, moved briefly to Zanesville, and then returned to Chillicothe until 1816, when Columbus became the permanent capital.

CHAPTER TWO

The State Constitution

A constitution is the fundamental law by which a state or nation is governed. Ohio's present constitution was approved by the electorate in 1851. Except for major amendments drawn by the Constitutional Convention of 1912 and individual amendments that have been adopted from time to time, it is today the same basic document drafted more than a century and a half ago.

The Ohio Constitution is the supreme law of the state, subject only to the Constitution of the United States and federal laws and treaties. The constitution can only be changed by approval of a majority of the electors voting on a proposed amendment. All statutes passed by the legislature, and rules and regulations of the various departments of state government, must conform to the Ohio Constitution.

All powers not granted to the federal government or prohibited by the U.S. Constitution reside with the states or the people. The Ohio Constitution divides those powers not reserved by the people among three branches of the state government: the legislative, the executive, and the judicial. The legislature makes the laws, the executive branch administers and enforces them, and the judiciary interprets their meaning. In addition, Ohio, like all other states and the federal government itself, employs a system of checks and balances to ensure that any one branch's power does not supersede the power of the others.

The rights of the individual are enumerated in Article I of the Ohio Constitution; they are known as the Ohio Bill of Rights and are similar to the Bill of Rights contained in the first ten amendments to the U.S. Constitution. Citizens have the right to freedom of speech, press, assembly, and worship; they are entitled to fair and equal treatment in the courts; and they are protected from unreasonable search and seizure. The importance of these freedoms is emphasized by their inclusion by those who adopted the first state constitution, even though they were already guaranteed by the first ten amendments to the United States Constitution.

Other articles of the Ohio Constitution define the organization, powers, and responsibilities of the three branches of state government. The articles deal with elections, education, public institutions, public debt, public works, the militia, county and township organization, apportionment, finance and taxation, corporations, municipal corporations, and the methods of amending the constitution.

Amending the Ohio Constitution

There are three ways to amend the Ohio Constitution: proposal by the General Assembly; proposal by the people through an initiative petition; and by constitutional convention. In all cases, proposals must be submitted to the voters and approved by a majority of those citizens voting on them to become part of the state constitution.

The first method to amend the constitution is for a member of either house of the General Assembly to propose an amendment to the constitution. If three-fifths of the members of each house agree to the proposed amendment, it is submitted to the voters. If a majority of citizens voting approves the question, it becomes part of the constitution.

The second way that the Ohio Constitution may be amended is by the people through the initiative process. A description of initiative petition can be found in Chapter 11.

The third way to amend the constitution is through a constitutional convention. A convention may submit its proposals as separate amendments or may submit a totally new constitution to the electorate for adoption or rejection. This method has only been used three times: 1802, 1851, and 1912. Every 20 years voters must decide if "a convention to revise, alter, or amend the constitution" should be called.

The question of calling a convention may be placed on the ballot at any time by a vote of two-thirds of the members of each house of the General Assembly. If a majority of those citizens voting on the question favor the calling of a convention, the legislature must arrange for the election of delegates and the assembling of the convention. The voters of Ohio rejected the opportunity to call a convention in 1932, 1952, 1972, and again in 1992. In November 2012, the voters will again decide on whether or not to call for a constitutional convention.

OHIO'S THREE BRANCHES OF GOVERNMENT

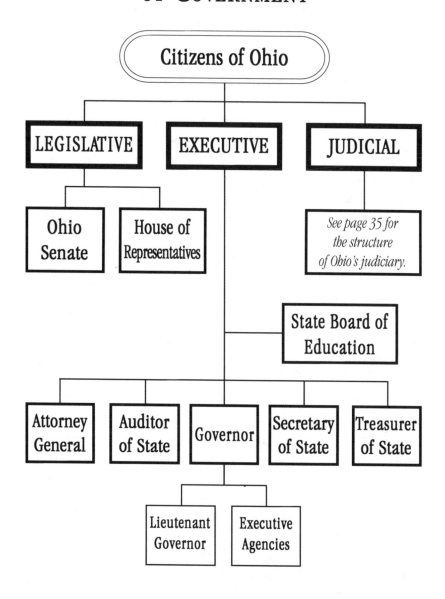

Source: Ohio Public Library Information Network

CHAPTER THREE

The Legislature

A legislature is a body of individuals elected by the people to enact laws on behalf of the citizens. Ohio citizens have legislative representation at the national and state levels. The United States Congress is the federal legislative body, and the Ohio General Assembly is the state legislative body. Local legislative representation in Ohio is dependent on the local government structure. Each level of representation has the power to enact laws that fall within its jurisdiction. Congress enacts federal laws, and the Ohio General Assembly enacts state laws. The laws enacted by Congress cannot violate the U.S. Constitution, and the Ohio General Assembly cannot pass laws that conflict with the U.S. or Ohio constitutions. In addition to representing citizens, the U.S. Congress and the Ohio General Assembly have the duty to impeach and oust members of the executive branch who have committed certain crimes while in office.

Beyond legislative representation, Ohio citizens have the constitutional right to propose state laws themselves through the initiative process.

Representation—Federal

The United States Congress is a bicameral legislature—that is, it comprises two houses or chambers: the U.S. Senate and the U.S. House of Representatives. The 100-member Senate is made up of two senators from each state. The 435 seats in the U.S. House of Representatives are allocated to the states based on their populations as compared to the total U.S. population, but every state is entitled to at least one representative. Congressional seats are divided among the 50 states after each federal decennial census. In 2000, Ohio's population entitled it to 18 representatives for the following ten years. This represents a reduction by one representative, as Ohio's population has declined in proportion to the population of other states. The next federal census will be conducted in 2010.

The Ohio General Assembly is empowered to draw boundary lines for congressional districts through the regular legislative process. Districts must be substantially equal in population. There is no Ohio constitutional provision that prevents the General Assembly from redrawing the congressional districts between censuses. The current congressional district map, established in 2002 by the General Assembly, can be found on page 10.

U.S. senators serve for terms of six years, with one-third of the Senate elected every two years. Senators were originally chosen by the state legislatures, but with the passage of the Seventeenth Amendment to the U.S. Constitution, senators are directly elected by the voters. U.S. representatives are elected for two-year terms, all terms running for the same period. Both the senators and the representatives must be residents of the state from which they are chosen. In addition, a senator must be at least 30 years of age and must have been a citizen of the United States for at least nine years; a representative must be at least 25 years of age and must have been a citizen for at least seven years.

Although Ohio voters passed an amendment to the Ohio Constitution to enact term limits for federal- and state-level legislators, the U.S. Supreme Court ruled that term limits on federal-level representation are unconstitutional and voided this provision of the 1992 amendment.

Representation—State

The Ohio General Assembly is also a bicameral legislature, comprising the Ohio House of Representatives and the Ohio Senate. Ohio's system of determining state legislative representation was changed in the 1960s as a result of historic U.S. Supreme Court decisions. The Court required both houses of bicameral state legislatures to be apportioned on the basis of population alone. Ohio voters approved a state constitutional amendment that established the current method of districting in 1967.

Article XI of the Ohio Constitution establishes 99 districts for the Ohio House of Representatives and 33 districts for the Ohio Senate. All members of the General Assembly are elected from single-member districts of approximately equal populations. Each House member represents about 110,000 Ohioans, and each senator about 330,000. Because districts are drawn according to population, Ohio's urban centers have a larger number of representatives and senators compared to the rural areas. District boundaries are drawn every ten years, following the federal decennial census. A five-member Apportionment Board, made up of the governor, auditor of state, secretary of state, and one member from each of the major political parties selected by their respective legislative leaders, is charged with the task of establishing both Ohio House and Ohio Senate districts.

The Apportionment Board must follow guidelines that are specified in Article XI of the Ohio Constitution. House districts must be created by using

OHIO'S CONGRESSIONAL DISTRICTS
2002-2012

Courtesy of the Secretary of State's Office
For more information, visit http://www.sos.state.oh.us, select "Vote," then "District Maps"

the borders of political subdivisions (counties, cities, townships) and be "compact . . . contiguous . . . and [bound] by a single non-intersecting continuous line." There may be no more than a plus or minus five-percent population variance among districts. Senate districts are created by combining three contiguous House districts.

General Assembly

The term General Assembly refers both to the legislative body as a whole and to the two-year period that consists of two regular sessions that begin in January. The latter usage is usually preceded by a number to help differentiate among various two-year periods. The 125th General Assembly was in session in 2003-2004, the 126th General Assembly in 2005-2006, and so on.

The maps on pages 12 and 13 show the current Ohio House and Senate districts established in 2002. These districts will remain in effect until 2012, when the Apportionment Board will redraw General Assembly districts based on the 2010 census data.

To be eligible for office in the General Assembly, a person must have resided for one year in the district he or she seeks to represent. Ohio senators are elected for four-year terms, half of the senators being elected every two years. Representatives are elected for two-year terms. In 1992, voters passed an amendment to establish term limits for state level legislators. Members of the Ohio Senate may serve two consecutive four-year terms, and Ohio representatives may serve four consecutive two-year terms. After a waiting period of four years, former General Assembly members may seek reelection to their former office.

Organization of the General Assembly

A new legislative session is assembled every two years, following the November elections. Ohio's Constitution specifies that the General Assembly begin the first regular session on the first Monday of January in odd-numbered years, or on the succeeding day if the first Monday is a legal holiday. The second regular session must begin on the same date the following year. There is no limit to the length of the regular session. During the regular session, the legislature generally meets on Tuesdays, Wednesdays, and Thursdays. Neither chamber may adjourn for more than five days without the other chamber's consent.

The General Assembly Open Meetings Act ensures that all committee meetings of the General Assembly are open to the public. Full sessions of

OHIO'S STATE SENATE DISTRICTS

Courtesy of the Secretary of State's Office
For more information, visit http://www.sos.state.oh.us, select "Vote," then "District Maps"

OHIO'S STATE HOUSE DISTRICTS

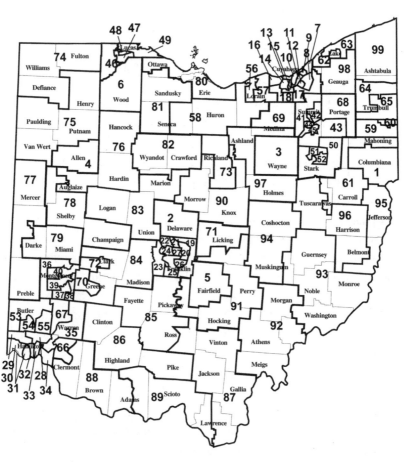

Courtesy of the Secretary of State's Office
For more information, visit http://www.sos.state.oh.us, select "Vote," then "District Maps"

either chamber are open to the public as well. However, the Ohio Constitution allows either chamber of the General Assembly to hold a closed session if two-thirds of the members present feel it necessary.

When the General Assembly is not in session, either the governor or the presiding officers of both houses acting together may call the legislature into special session by proclamation. The purpose of the special session is limited to the specific issues in the proclamation.

Each chamber of the General Assembly chooses its own officers to preside over the legislative process. Leadership positions exist for majority and minority party legislators. There are different numbers of officers in the House and Senate, bearing different titles, but generally, the functions remain the same across chamber lines.

Once each chamber has convened and selected officers, it draws up the rules it will follow during the coming two-year period. The rules establish procedures by which the members must abide. As well as establishing procedural rules, each chamber creates a system of punishment for members found to have disobeyed rules. Punishment can include expulsion from the legislature by a two-thirds vote of the House or Senate members. Each chamber publishes a record of proceedings in its journal.

Finally, each chamber establishes a series of legislative committees to examine legislation more thoroughly and to allow for an open public discussion on the merits of proposed legislation. The leadership in each chamber determines committee membership. The most common committees in the General Assembly are called standing committees and are considered permanent throughout the two-year session. Other temporary committees are established on an as-needed basis, including joint committees, which are made up of members from both the House and the Senate.

The standing committees often have subcommittees to hear testimony, amend bills or prepare substitute legislation, and report back to the standing committee with a recommendation. While the number and title of committees may vary from session to session, each chamber generally has standing committees to deal with matters related to agriculture, commerce, education, elections, environment, finance, health, transportation, the judiciary, labor, local government, public utilities, state government, taxation, and human resources. Each chamber has a rules committee, the primary job of which is to schedule bills for debate and/or vote on the floor of the chamber on any particular day. There is also a committee in each chamber that is responsible for referring bills to committee (see How a Bill Becomes Law on page 19) and eliminating frivolous or duplicate bills.

The political party that has the majority of elected members from its own party in each chamber traditionally has political control of the committees, and thus names the chair and receives a majority of the seats on the committee. Each senator and representative serves on several committees.

Procedures of the General Assembly

Once the chambers of the General Assembly have established an organization to begin a new, two-year legislative session, the members can engage in the business of the General Assembly: legislating.

There are two types of legislation considered in the General Assembly, bills and resolutions. A bill is a proposal introduced in the General Assembly that seeks to enact new laws, or to amend or repeal existing laws. Bills may originate in either house and may be altered, amended, or rejected in the other. The constitution requires that all bills must be considered by each chamber three different times, and that no bill may be passed until it has been reproduced and distributed to the members of that chamber. When committee hearings are held on bills, interested people may ask or be requested to testify before the committee either in support of or in opposition to the legislation being considered. This offers an opportunity for an individual or organization to make its wishes known directly to the legislators. After a bill has passed both houses of the General Assembly, it becomes an act, and once the act is signed by the governor and a 90-day waiting period passes, the act becomes law and is inserted into the Ohio Revised Code. Some acts are passed on an emergency basis and become law immediately after the governor signs them.

The other type of legislation the General Assembly may consider is called a resolution. Resolutions serve as formal expressions of the opinions and wishes of the General Assembly and do not require approval of the governor. There are three types of resolutions: joint resolutions, concurrent resolutions, and simple resolutions.

Joint resolutions are reserved for matters of great importance to the General Assembly. They are generally used to form joint legislative committees, propose amendments to the Ohio Constitution, petition Congress, and ratify amendments to the U.S. Constitution. A joint resolution must pass both houses and be filed with the secretary of state. Proposed amendments to the Ohio Constitution are placed on the ballot at the next general election for approval by Ohio's voters. Concurrent resolutions are generally used as statements of policy by the General Assembly to resolve internal procedural matters. Simple resolutions pertain to matters in either the House or the Senate and usually are issued to commemorate a person, group, or event, or to state policy of just one of the chambers.

The text below and chart on page 19 illustrate the path a bill must follow to become law in Ohio.

How Ohio Laws Are Made by the General Assembly

Introduction of a Bill

Ideas for bills come from various sources, including private citizens, interest groups, businesses, state agencies, and legislators. All bills proposed by a legislator must be reviewed by the Legislative Service Commission (LSC) for correct form before being introduced. A professional staff is employed by the LSC to draft bills and provide research services for members of the General Assembly. A bill must be sponsored by at least one legislator in order to be introduced in either house of the General Assembly. The Ohio Constitution also gives citizens the right to introduce legislation through the initiative petition process, although this is seldom done (see below). Any member of either house may introduce a bill, and that legislator becomes the bill's primary sponsor. Other legislators may sign as cosponsors. The primary sponsor manages the bill throughout the legislative process.

Bills are introduced on the floor of either chamber by reading the titles of the bills. Bills are filed with the legislative clerk, who assigns each a number to be used throughout the legislative process in both houses. House bills are numbered HB 1, HB 2, and so on; Senate bills are SB 1, SB 2, and so on. Introduction constitutes the first of the three considerations of each bill required by the Ohio Constitution.

The Ohio Revised Code

The Ohio Revised Code (ORC) is the collection of Ohio laws, rules, and regulations organized by subject matter. References to the Ohio Revised Code are cited as numbers that represent the chapter and section where the law, rule, or regulation can be found. For example, ORC citation 3501.01 refers to the chapter (35) and section (01) and article (.01) of the law that establishes definitions used in election law.

Referral

After introduction, the bill is sent to either the Rules and Reference Committee in the House or the Reference Committee in the Senate, where it is reviewed and normally assigned to a standing committee for testimony, debate, and committee action. The referral of a bill to a committee is the second consideration of the bill.

Committee Hearings and Action

An important part of the legislative process takes place in committee, where the fate of a bill is usually determined. The committee examines and debates those bills assigned to it. Complex or controversial issues are often referred to a subcommittee for more thorough consideration or redrafting. The committee can either begin processing the bill or take no action, which essentially defeats the bill for the remainder of the session. If a committee wishes to take action on a bill, hearings are scheduled. In most cases at least two hearings are held on a bill, one for proponents and one for opponents. The committee may amend, rewrite, or combine bills based on testimony gathered at public hearings conducted by the committee. The committee then votes either to report the bill favorably for consideration by the entire chamber or to postpone the legislation indefinitely, which defeats the bill. The consent of a majority of the committee members is required to take either action.

Rules Committees

Bills that have been favorably reported out by a standing committee are sent to the rules committee of that chamber. Each rules committee creates a calendar that lists when bills will be considered for debate and a full vote by the entire membership of the House or the Senate. This is important because only bills that are on the calendar can be voted upon. The rules committees have the power to prevent floor action on a bill by never scheduling a bill on the calendar.

Full Chamber Consideration

The bills sent to the entire chamber are given a third consideration in the order listed on the calendar. The bill's sponsor begins the discussion by giving a review of the bill's purpose and content. Bills are then debated and amended according to the procedures of each chamber. All members present are required to vote unless they have gained permission in advance to abstain due to conflict of interest. The Ohio House votes through an electronic roll call system. The Ohio Senate calls the roll by voice. The bill can be passed, defeated, or postponed until later. To pass, a bill must attain a favorable vote by a simple majority of the membership, 50 votes in the House and 17 in the Senate. Emergency legislation—that is, a bill that contains language that would make it effective immediately upon approval by the governor—requires a two-thirds majority vote. A bill enacting a constitutional amendment requires a three-fifths majority to be put before the voters.

After a bill passes one chamber, it is sent to the other, where it follows a similar procedure. If a bill is modified by the second chamber, it must be returned to the first chamber for approval of the changes. Both houses must approve the same version of the bill.

If the first chamber rejects the modifications, the second chamber may request that a conference committee be established to produce a version that both houses will approve. The conference committee comprises three members from each chamber. Once the committee has produced a compromise bill, both houses must then vote to accept the conference committee version. If the committee cannot reach an agreement acceptable to both houses, the bill is defeated.

The Governor

A bill that has passed both houses is enrolled, printed in final form as an act , and signed by both the speaker of the House and the president of the Senate. The act is then transmitted to the governor, who has ten days to take action. If the governor approves, the bill is signed and the act becomes law in 90 days unless otherwise specified in its provisions. Emergency or appropriation measures become effective immediately. If the governor does not approve of the legislation, it is vetoed and returned to the house of origin with the governor's written objections. Appropriation bills can be vetoed on a line-by-line basis, whereas other types of legislation can be vetoed only as a whole. A three-fifths majority vote is required in both houses to override a veto. If the governor fails either to sign or veto the act by the end of ten days (excluding Sundays), it becomes law following the same time lines as if it had been signed.

> # The Chances of a Bill Becoming a Law . . .
>
> *The legislative process in Ohio is complex; the bill must pass both the Senate and House of Representatives and be signed by the governor. In the 124th session of the General Assembly, only 25 percent of the total bills introduced in the General Assembly became law.*

HOW A BILL BECOMES A LAW IN OHIO

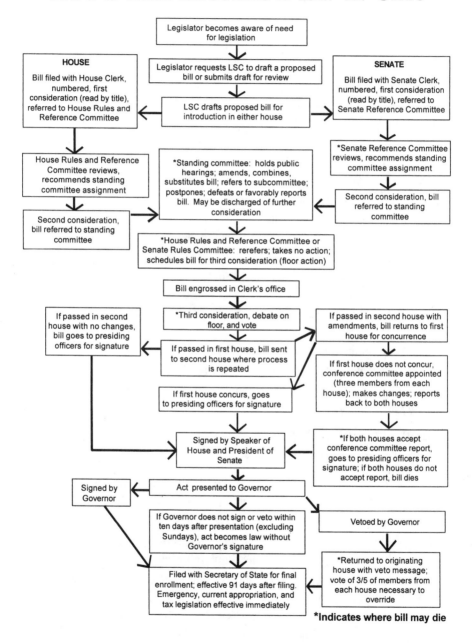

Legislator becomes aware of need for legislation

HOUSE
Bill filed with House Clerk, numbered, first consideration (read by title), referred to House Rules and Reference Committee

Legislator requests LSC to draft a proposed bill or submits draft for review

SENATE
Bill filed with Senate Clerk, numbered, first consideration (read by title), referred to Senate Reference Committee

LSC drafts proposed bill for introduction in either house

House Rules and Reference Committee reviews, recommends standing committee assignment

*Standing committee: holds public hearings; amends, combines, substitutes bill; refers to subcommittee; postpones; defeats or favorably reports bill. May be discharged of further consideration

*Senate Reference Committee reviews, recommends standing committee assignment

Second consideration, bill referred to standing committee

Second consideration, bill referred to standing committee

*House Rules and Reference Committee or Senate Rules Committee: rerefers; takes no action; schedules bill for third consideration (floor action)

Bill engrossed in Clerk's office

If passed in second house with no changes, bill goes to presiding officers for signature

*Third consideration, debate on floor, and vote

If passed in second house with amendments, bill returns to first house for concurrence

If passed in first house, bill sent to second house where process is repeated

If first house does not concur, conference committee appointed (three members from each house); makes changes; reports back to both houses

If first house concurs, goes to presiding officers for signature

Signed by Speaker of House and President of Senate

*If both houses accept conference committee report, goes to presiding officers for signature; if both houses do not accept report, bill dies

Signed by Governor

Act presented to Governor

If Governor does not sign or veto within ten days after presentation (excluding Sundays), act becomes law without Governor's signature

Vetoed by Governor

*Returned to originating house with veto message; vote of 3/5 of members from each house necessary to override

Filed with Secretary of State for final enrollment; effective 91 days after filing. Emergency, current appropriation, and tax legislation effective immediately

*Indicates where bill may die

Source: Ohio Legislative Service Commission, A Guidebook for Ohio Legislators, *Eighth Edition*

Legislative Service Commission

A 14-member Legislative Service Commission (LSC) was created by statute in 1953 to assist the legislature in a variety of ways. The commission is made up of the speaker of the House and six members of the House appointed by the speaker, and the president of the Senate and six members of the Senate appointed by the president. No more than four members from each house may be of the same political party.

The staff includes a director, appointed by and serving at the pleasure of the commission, and a full-time staff organized into sections according to subject matter. The staff is responsible for drafting bills, amendments, resolutions, and letters of commendation requested by legislators; serving as staff for committees of the General Assembly; and preparing analyses, fiscal notes, and local impact statements of bills considered in committee or on the floor of the House or Senate.

In addition, the LSC staff writes research memoranda and reports on a wide variety of topics as requested and provides estimates of state revenue. The commission also conducts long-term project research as required by statute or by resolution of the 14-member LSC and codifies both the laws of Ohio and the administrative rules adopted by state agencies.

The LSC staff operates a library that provides services to members of the General Assembly and the general public.

The staff also publishes *Members Only* briefs, *Budget Footnotes*, *Ohio Facts*, the *Digest of Enactments*, status reports of legislation, and a *Guidebook for Ohio Legislators*.

Joint Legislative Ethics Committee/Office of the Legislative Inspector General

The Joint Legislative Ethics Committee (JLEC) was established by the Ohio General Assembly in 1994 to monitor compliance with Ohio's ethics law as it applies to the legislative branch. The committee consists of no more than 12 members, six from each party and six from each legislative body. JLEC is responsible for administering Ohio's lobbying laws and exercises its powers and duties pertaining to lobbyists and their employers. Ohio law requires all paid lobbyists, or persons engaged in influencing legislation during at least a part of their time, to register with the Joint Legislative Ethic Committee (JLEC). Influencing legislation is defined as occurring when direct communication is made with a legislator or executive official. Volunteer lobbyists and those lobbying on their own behalf need not register.

Employers of paid lobbyists must also register, and both employers and paid lobbyists must indicate the type of legislation in which they are interested. In Ohio, there is a small fee for registering. JLEC issues a card to lobbyists showing that they have registered. Lobbyists are required to file a statement of expenditures three times a year.

The Office of the Legislative Inspector General (OLIG) is accountable to the Joint Legislative Ethics Committee and is responsible for the actual implementation of the provisions of the ethics and lobbying laws. OLIG was created by executive order in 1988. In 1990, the General Assembly approved legislation making OLIG permanent.

Joint Committee on Agency Rule Review

The Joint Committee on Agency Rule Review (JCARR) is a joint legislative committee comprising five state senators and five state representatives. The primary function of JCARR is to review proposed administrative rules to ensure that the rule: 1) does not exceed the statutory authority of the agency; 2) is consistent with legislative intent; 3) does not conflict with another administrative rule; and 4) is accompanied by a complete and accurate rule summary and fiscal analysis. If the rule fails in any one of the above categories, JCARR may recommend the adoption of a concurrent resolution by the General Assembly.

Legislative Activism

JCARR offers a listserv service so that constituents can receive weekly summaries and agendas via e-mail. See http://www.jcarr.state.oh.us.

Legislative Information Office

The Legislative Information Office was created by the General Assembly in 1973 to assist the public in contacting legislators and obtaining basic legislative information. The office provides information about the status of bills, the schedule of legislative committee hearings, and the agendas for the Ohio House of Representatives and the Ohio Senate calendars; assists callers with locating documents and other information available on the legislative Web site; matches callers with their elected officials when that information is unknown; and takes messages for legislators. Calls are answered Monday through Friday from 8:30 a.m. to 5 p.m. The telephone number for Columbus-area callers is (614) 466-8842; callers from other areas of Ohio may call toll-free, 1-800-282-0253.

Legislative Office of Education Oversight

The Ohio Legislative Office of Education Oversight (LOEO) was created in 1989 to serve as a nonpartisan staff to the ten-member Legislative Committee on Education Oversight. LOEO evaluates primary, secondary, and post-secondary education programs that receive funds from the state of Ohio.

Capitol Square Review and Advisory Board

The Capitol Square Review and Advisory Board is responsible for maintaining the historical character of the Statehouse and Capitol Square while providing for the health, safety, and convenience of those who work in or visit the complex. The Capitol Square Review and Advisory Board consists of 11 members. There are four members from the General Assembly, two from the Ohio Senate and two from the Ohio House. There are five board members appointed by the governor representing the Ohio Department of Administrative Services, the Ohio Building Authority, the Ohio Arts Council, the Ohio Historical Society, and the general public. A former speaker of the Ohio House of Representatives is appointed by the sitting speaker to sit on the board, and a former president of the Ohio Senate is appointed by the sitting president. The Capitol Square Review and Advisory Board, through a cooperative effort with the Ohio Historical Society, coordinates tours of the Statehouse and provides information about the buildings, their history, and Ohio's government.

Correctional Institution Inspection Committee

The eight member Correctional Institution Inspection Committee is charged with inspecting each state correctional institution every two years. The committee consists of four members each from the House of Representatives and the Senate, with both major parties being equally represented. Appointments to the committee are made by the speaker of the House of Representatives and the president of the Senate. The committee is served by four staff members. Members attend one meal as well as one rehabilitative or educational program without advance notice to ensure quality throughout the correctional facilities. Inspection of grievance procedures is required as well. A report to the General Assembly follows each two-year inspection. The administrative staff office closed during fiscal year 2003 due to financial constraints. However, it was reopened during fiscal year 2004.

CHAPTER FOUR

The Judiciary

The Ohio Constitution guarantees to all citizens certain basic rights. In the pursuit of these rights disputes may arise—between individuals, between a person and the government, or between agencies of government. The judicial branch, or court system, is the arm of the government that provides a means to settle these disputes. It interprets the laws set forth by the Ohio Constitution or those enacted by the legislature. It is independent of both the executive and legislative branches in order to protect the legal rights of the people and guarantee equal protection under the law for everyone.

The Ohio Constitution established three courts to administer judicial powers: the Ohio Supreme Court, the Court of Appeals, and the Court of Common Pleas. These three courts cannot be abolished except through amendment of the Ohio Constitution. In addition to these constitutional courts, the Ohio Constitution allows the legislature to create other courts to assist the Court of Common Pleas. These are called statutory courts because they can be created or abolished by the legislature. The legislature has estab-

---

Voting for Judges in Ohio

To avoid the possibility that voters will elect candidates based on promises made about specific court cases, judicial candidates must remain nonpartisan after the primary election campaign and should at all times refrain from making comments that might indicate how they would rule on certain issues. This rule is spelled out in the Judicial Canons:

> *"Canon 7 – A judge should refrain from political activity inappropriate to [one's] judicial office . . . [and] . . . should not make pledges or promises of conduct in office other than the faithful and impartial performance of the duties of the office; announce [one's] views on disputed legal or political issues; or misrepresent [one's] identity, qualifications, present position, or other fact."*

lished municipal courts, county courts, mayor's courts, and the Ohio Court of Claims.

Courts are charged with settling disputes rather than mediating between parties. As such, Ohio statute does not prescribe mediation courts. Mediation is a voluntary process involving a neutral third party, called a mediator, who assists adversaries such as those in a civil lawsuit in resolving a complaint in a manner acceptable to both parties. Various courts in Ohio may have mediation programs, just as some have drug courts. But these programs exist only within the jurisdiction of the court that created them and have no statutory powers.

Ohio's court procedures are based on the adversary system. Both sides in a dispute have the opportunity to present their arguments before a court of law. Two types of cases come before the courts: civil and criminal. Civil cases involve debts, contracts, property rights, and other matters not defined as criminal. Criminal cases are classified as either felonies or misdemeanors. Felonies, for example, include murder, manslaughter, kidnapping, and burglary. Misdemeanor cases usually involve traffic violations and disturbing the peace. A court may have either original jurisdiction (beginning of a case through to a decision) or appellate jurisdiction (review of a lower court's decision), or it may have both jurisdictions in different cases.

Ohio's constitutional courts and the statutory courts, with the exception of mayor's courts, are courts of record. This means that the proceedings of these courts are kept as a perpetual record of what has taken place in each court, including the process, pleadings, reports, verdicts, transcripts, orders, and judgments. Appeals are based on the records kept by the courts.

Constitutional Courts

The Supreme Court

The Ohio Supreme Court consists of a chief justice and six justices; the number of justices can be changed by statute. Its primary concern is with cases that consider a substantial constitutional question. The Ohio Supreme Court is the court of final judicial review in the state. It must accept appeals of cases that originated in the courts of appeals; cases involving the death penalty; cases involving questions arising under the U.S. Constitution or the Ohio Constitution; and cases in which there have been conflicting opinions from two or more courts of appeals. The Ohio Supreme Court acts as a check on the legislative and executive branches through its review of the constitutionality of laws and its review of actions of executive agencies. It provides uniformity in the application of the laws of the state through its review process and is the final authority in the state on matters of law.

The Ohio Supreme Court exercises general supervision over all courts. This power is exercised by the chief justice, who oversees courts in the state according to rules set by the Supreme Court. An administrative director and staff assist the chief justice. Rules governing practices and procedures in all courts are prepared by the Supreme Court and may be filed with the clerk of each house of the General Assembly by the 15th of January of any year. The rules take effect July 1 unless both houses of the General Assembly adopt a concurrent resolution of disapproval. After adoption of a rule, all laws in conflict with it are of no further force. Rules of civil, criminal, appellate, and juvenile procedure have been adopted in this manner, as well as evidence rules. Lower courts may adopt additional rules concerning local practice, providing they are consistent with the statewide rules prepared by the Supreme Court.

The Supreme Court also adopts administrative rules that apply to all courts. These rules of superintendence deal with assignment of judges, disqualification of judges, uniform record keeping, admission to the practice of law, and discipline of persons practicing law in the state. Rules of superintendence are effective immediately upon adoption by the Supreme Court. Only rules of practice and procedure are subject to legislative review. Any rule promulgated by the Supreme Court cannot enlarge, modify, or abridge any substantive right.

The Supreme Court administers the Client Security Fund. Established in 1985, it is a fund for reimbursing clients for losses due to theft or fraud by their lawyers. The Client Security Fund is funded by a portion of the attorney registration fees assessed to each practicing attorney in Ohio every two years.

The Supreme Court meets in Columbus year round. Supreme Court justices serve six-year terms. Candidates are nominated in party primaries or may file nominating petitions as independent candidates; they run in the general election on a nonpartisan ballot. They must be attorneys admitted to practice law in Ohio and have at least six years' experience in the practice of law in the state or six years as a judge in any state.

Court of Appeals

Although the courts of appeals have original jurisdiction in certain specified cases, the primary responsibility of courts of appeals is to hear appeals from the common pleas, county, and municipal courts. They review orders and actions of administrative officers or agencies through an appeal from the common pleas court. Cases are heard and decided by a panel of three appellate judges.

Ohio is divided into 12 appellate districts. Each district is served by a court of appeals that can sit in any county in that district, if circumstances warrant it. The court districts vary in size depending on population and workload. Cuyahoga, Franklin, and Hamilton counties are single-county districts. The 10th District Court of Appeals in Franklin County also hears appeals from the Ohio Court of Claims.

The number of judges in an appellate district depends on caseload and district size, but there is a minimum of three judges per district. Additional judges may be added to any district by the legislature when circumstances require it. In districts with more than three judges, any three may act as a court of appeals panel. There are currently 68 Ohio Court of Appeals judges.

Court of appeals judges serve six-year terms. They may be nominated in party primaries but run in the general election on a nonpartisan ballot. A candidate may also file as an independent candidate under the rules set forth for independent candidates in the Ohio Revised Code. Court of appeals judges must be admitted to practice as an attorney at law in Ohio and have practiced law in Ohio for at least six years, or have been a judge in any state for at least six years.

Court of Common Pleas

The constitution provides for a court of common pleas to serve each of the 88 counties in the state. Courts of common pleas have original jurisdiction in felonies and in civil cases where the amount in dispute is greater than $500. Common pleas courts have appellate jurisdiction over most state agencies.

Three specialized divisions of the court of common pleas have been established to decide cases involving probate, domestic, and juvenile matters; however, these divisions may not be present as separate entities in every county.

Probate courts have jurisdiction over the probate of wills and supervise the administration of estates and guardianships. They are responsible for overseeing adoption proceedings, issuing marriage licenses, and ruling on cases involving questions of mental competency or physical disability. Probate judges are allowed to perform marriages as well.

Courts of domestic relations handle divorce, dissolution of marriage, spousal support, spousal abuse, annulment, separation, and allocation of parental rights and responsibilities for the care of children. Each court works in conjunction with a local child support enforcement agency to handle support enforcement.

OHIO COURT OF APPEALS DISTRICTS

Courtesy of the Secretary of State's Office

Juvenile courts hear cases involving people under 18 years of age who have been charged with acts that would be crimes if committed by an adult. The juvenile court has authority in cases involving unruly, dependent, or neglected children. Juvenile courts have jurisdiction in adult cases that involve matters of paternity, child abuse, nonsupport, contributing to the delinquency of a minor, or failure to send children to school. However, 14- to 17-year-olds who are accused of committing a felony offense and who are not amenable to rehabilitation in the juvenile system may be transferred, or bound over, to adult court.

Retired judges of any court may accept civil cases on an assignment basis. This means that they may hear cases in the courts of common pleas, the municipal courts, and the court of claims. The retired judges are assigned cases by the chief justice of the Ohio Supreme Court.

Every judge must file monthly and annual reports with the chief justice covering the number of cases assigned, those pending, and those terminated. The administrative judge reviews the reports of all judges in the division.

Statutes, case law, local court rules, Ohio rules of criminal and civil procedure, and the Ohio Rules of Superintendence provide for the disposition of civil and criminal cases filed.

Recommendations of the Ohio Courts Futures Commission

In 2000, the Ohio Courts Futures Commission, a 52-member committee charged with examining the state judicial system, made a number of recommendations for reforming the judiciary by 2025. The commission delivered recommendations for meeting the needs of Ohioans for the long term. The commission recommended modifying court hours of operation; increasing the availability of legal aid attorneys, appointed counsel, and other affordable sources of legal assistance to low- income families; and providing more information to the community in nontechnical language. Some of the other reforms included establishing technological uniformity among the courts, reorganizing county courts to improve efficiency, expanding sources for jury pools, and replacing mayor's courts with trained judicial officials.

The number of judges assigned to the common pleas court of a county varies according to population. Common pleas judges are elected for six-year terms. They may be nominated in partisan primaries or may file nominating petitions as independent candidates. They then run on nonpartisan judicial ballots in the general election. They must be a resident of Ohio, be admitted to practice law in Ohio, and have practiced law in the state for at least six years or have been a judge in any state for that amount of time.

Statutory Courts

Municipal Courts

Municipal courts are courts of record with preliminary hearing jurisdiction in felony cases and original jurisdiction in traffic and criminal misdemeanor cases committed within the court's jurisdictional territory. Civil cases are also heard in municipal court as long as the amount in controversy does not exceed $15,000, except for cases in the housing or environmental division, where there is no dollar limit. Municipal courts may establish small claims divisions that handle civil cases where the dollar amount does not exceed $3,000.

Marriage and the Courts

When justices of the peace were eliminated by Ohio law, municipal and county courts took over their duties. Therefore, judges sitting in these courts have the authority to perform marriages.

Territorial jurisdiction for each municipal court in Ohio is established by statute; many have county-wide jurisdiction. Standard uniform rules for superintendence of municipal courts, similar to those for common pleas courts, were established in 1975 by the Supreme Court.

Judges are nominated by partisan primary or nominating petition and are elected on a nonpartisan judicial ballot unless a city charter establishes a different procedure. They are elected for six-year terms and serve full- or part-time as provided by statute. Municipal court judges must be admitted to practice law in Ohio and have practiced law in the state for at least six years or have been a judge in any state for six years.

County Courts

County courts were established in 1957 for counties where municipal courts do not have county-wide jurisdiction. They can have territorial jurisdiction in all areas of the county not served by municipal courts. They are courts of record and exercise the same criminal jurisdiction as municipal courts, and can establish small claims divisions as well. County court judges serve six-year terms and are nominated by petition only. They must be admitted to practice law in Ohio and have engaged in the practice of law for six years preceding their nomination.

Mayor's Courts

In general, Ohio law allows mayors of municipal corporations populated by more than 100 people where there is no municipal court to conduct mayor's court. These courts hear only cases involving violations of local ordinances and state traffic laws.

Mayor's courts are not courts of record but must file statistics quarterly and annually with the Supreme Court. Additionally, at the request of the General Assembly, the Supreme Court has adopted rules providing for court procedures and basic legal education for mayors. Mayors whose courts hear alcohol- and drug-related traffic offenses have additional requirements.

A mayor is not required to be a lawyer, but may appoint an attorney who has engaged in the practice of law for three years to hear cases in mayor's court.

A person convicted in a mayor's court having jurisdiction within the municipal corporation may appeal the decision to a municipal or county court.

Court of Claims

The Court of Claims has statewide original jurisdiction in all civil actions against the state of Ohio and its agencies. Cases may include matters involving personal injury, property damage, or contract actions. The Court of Claims was established by the General Assembly in 1976. The court sits in Franklin County, but the chief justice may order the court to sit in any county to hear a case if circumstances warrant it. Incumbent and retired judges temporarily assigned by the chief justice of the Ohio Supreme Court sit on the Court of Claims.

Civil actions brought before the Court of Claims are decided by one of two methods. Actions of less than $2,500 are decided administratively by the clerk or deputy clerk. Actions of more than $2,500 are decided by a single judge or, in the case of a complex law, by a three-judge panel. Juries are not used in deciding cases that come before the Court of Claims.

In 1976 the Ohio Victims of Crime Compensation Program was established, to be administered by the Court of Claims under the guidance of Ohio's chief justice. The purpose of the Ohio Victims of Crime Compensation Program is to grant compensation to a person injured or killed as a victim of crime or while preventing a crime, apprehending a criminal, or assisting a police officer. Victims of drunk drivers became eligible for compensation in 1989.

The Ohio Victims of Crime Compensation Program provides a way for victims or dependents of deceased victims to receive compensation for certain crime-related expenses, including medical and rehabilitation expenses, payment for lost wages, psychological counseling, funeral expenses, and the cost of services the victim normally would perform but now must pay someone else to perform. The maximum compensation is $50,000 per victim per incident. The program is funded by extra charges on court costs from felony and misdemeanor convictions and pleas (excluding non-moving traffic violations) as well as on the reinstatement of a driver's license pursuant to a drunk driving conviction.

Applications for compensation are available from the Court of Claims, all county common pleas courts, and most law enforcement agencies. To be eligible, the victim must report the crime within 72 hours and must file an application within two years at any common pleas court or the Court of Claims. After the Court of Claims receives the application, it is investigated by the Office of the Ohio Attorney General, which makes a recommendation to the court. A single commissioner of the court makes the decision on each claim. Commissioners, who must be attorneys licensed to practice law in Ohio, are appointed by and serve at the pleasure of the Supreme Court. The decision can be appealed, by either the applicant or the state of Ohio, to the court's panel of commissioners, and from there to a judge of the Court of Claims. The judge's decision is final.

The Jury System

"In any trial, in any court, the party accused shall be allowed . . . to have . . . a speedy public trial by an impartial jury of the county in which the offense is alleged to have been committed." Section 10, Article 1 of the Ohio Constitution guarantees the right to trial by jury. Trials are first held in courts of original jurisdiction (common pleas, municipal, county). Two types of juries are used in the Ohio court system, the grand jury and the petit (pronounced *PET-it*) jury.

In most cases, a grand jury investigates cases before a suspect is arrested and decides whether the accused should be indicted. It hears criminal cases to determine whether the accused should be held for trial. It does not make final judgment of guilt, and its proceedings are secret. The prosecutor's role is to present cases, question witnesses, and make recommendations. The prosecutor does not hear the jury's deliberations. The grand jury consists of nine members selected at random either from the registered voters in the county or from a list of licensed drivers. Seven members must concur in order to bring an indictment.

A petit jury is used in both criminal and civil cases and is the jury system most commonly associated with a trial. In criminal cases, the jury determines the guilt or innocence of the accused; in civil cases, it determines liability. Both parties present evidence and the jury decides the verdict based on the evidence and the instructions from the judge about the law of the case. Criminal defendants are presumed innocent unless shown to be guilty beyond a reasonable doubt. In civil cases, a lesser threshold must be met, with liability assigned using what is known as a preponderance, or majority, of the evidence. The number of petit jurors depends on the case. Juries hearing criminal cases are composed of 12 members for felonies and eight members for misdemeanors. The verdict must be unanimous. Eight-member juries hear civil cases unless both parties agree to a lesser number. Two-thirds of the members must concur in the verdict rendered in a civil case.

Special rules govern procedures in juvenile courts, of which the most noteworthy is that the accused does not have the right to a jury trial and that juvenile records can be sealed or expunged. There are also separate rules for traffic cases.

Sentencing

Sentencing laws are established to punish offenders and to protect the public. The state uses both incarceration and rehabilitation to achieve these goals. In the late 1980s, Ohio faced a growing prison population, resulting in crowded facilities and fewer resources. To address this concern, the Ohio General Assembly established the Ohio Criminal Sentencing Commission in 1990 to restructure Ohio's sentencing laws. The felony sentencing laws adopted in 1996 mean longer prison terms for many violent offenders, with more nonviolent offenders in local rehabilitation programs.

The commission has condensed the number of adult offense classifications to the following (listed in order of seriousness): aggravated murder, murder, felony one through felony five, misdemeanor one through misdemeanor four, and minor misdemeanor. Sentencing guidelines, found in the Ohio Revised Code, establish a range of prison and jail terms for each crime level. If a judge sentences a person to state prison or local jail, he or she must select a *specific* term from the ranges. In sentencing a felon to prison, the judge must include post-release control. Post-release control replaced parole for those sentenced after June 1996. The Parole Board no longer decides when to release inmates sentenced to prison after that date. The judge instead sets the actual term at sentencing.

Penalties for the most serious offenses include life in prison or death. State prison terms are mandatory for murderers, rapists, higher-level drug offenders, and those who use firearms or repeat serious offenses. Prison terms are presumed for other serious offenses. Judges may also impose fines and order supervision after the offender's release from prison.

For less serious felonies and most misdemeanors, trial judges have more discretion in imposing a sentence that is appropriate to the crime and circumstances of the case. This spectrum of options includes state prison (for felons only), community-based facility terms, fines, house arrest, community service, drug and alcohol use monitoring, supervision by community officials, and curfew, to name a few. These options are designed to shift some of the burden of dealing with nonviolent offenders from state prisons to community programs. State funding is provided to administer these programs, since generally the cost is less than housing the offender in a state prison or local jail.

"Minor misdemeanors" are the least serious offenses. They are also the most common offenses, since most traffic infractions (at least on first offense) fall under this category. No prison or jail term is imposed for minor misdemeanors. While the court typically imposes a fine for these offenses, since January 2004, they also have the option to impose community service work and even restitution if there is property damage to the victim.

The chief justice of the Ohio Supreme Court chairs the 31-member Criminal Sentencing Commission. The chair nominates ten members of the commission, including one judge from the Court of Appeals, three municipal or county judges, and three common pleas judges. The governor appoints 12 members, including a county, juvenile, and municipal prosecutor; two defense attorneys; an Ohio State Bar Association representative; a sheriff; two police chiefs; a crime victim; a county commissioner; and a mayor. Four members of the General Assembly serve on the commission as well, two from each party and two from each house. Furthermore, the state public defender, the director of the Department of Rehabilitation and Correction, the director of the Department of Youth Services, and the superintendent of the Highway Patrol are members of the commission.

Board of Commissioners on Grievances and Discipline

The Board of Commissioners on Grievances and Discipline of the Ohio Supreme Court conducts hearings, preserves the record, and makes findings and recommendations to the Supreme Court in disciplinary cases involving ethical misconduct charges brought against Ohio attorneys or judges. In addition, the board also issues advisory opinions on ethical issues affecting lawyers and judges statewide and serves as the statewide ethics agency for judges and magistrates. The board consists of 28 members appointed to three-year terms by the Supreme Court. The members include 17 attorneys, seven active or retired judges, and four non-attorneys.

Ohio Judicial Conference

The Ohio Judicial Conference is an agency in the judicial branch of government that works with Ohio judges to improve the administration of justice. Through the Judicial Conference, judges provide the General Assembly with analyses of the judicial impact of proposed legislation and with other information that is important to the legislative process. Through Judicial Conference committees, judges work on issues ranging from recommending improvements to jury service to informing judges about developments in court technology to helping judges develop programs to educate the public about the functioning of Ohio's judicial system.

All Ohio judges are members of the Judicial Conference, and many serve on Judicial Conference committees dealing with issues of concern to the judiciary. Five judges serve as officers of the Judicial Conference and guide the work of an executive director and professional staff of ten. The Judicial Conference offices are located in the Ohio Judicial Center in Columbus.

Board of Bar Examiners

The Board of Bar Examiners prepares and conducts examinations of applicants for admission to practice law in Ohio. The Ohio Supreme Court appoints members of the Board of Bar Examiners.

THE OHIO COURT SYSTEM

SUPREME COURT

Chief Justice and six justices

Court of last resort on state constitutional questions and questions of public or great general interest; appeals from the Board of Tax Appeals and Public Utilities Commission; all death sentences; and original jurisdiction in select cases.

COURTS OF APPEALS

Twelve districts, three-judge panels

Appellate review of judgments of common pleas, municipal and county courts; appeals from the Board of Tax Appeals; original jurisdiction in select cases.

COURTS OF COMMON PLEAS

In each of 88 counties

GENERAL DIVISION	DOMESTIC RELATIONS	PROBATE DIVISION	JUVENILE DIVISION
Civil and criminal cases; appeals from most administrative agencies	Divorces and dissolutions; support and custody of children	Decedents' estates; mental illness; adoptions; marriage licenses and weddings	Offenses involving minors; most paternity actions

MUNICIPAL COURTS

Misdemeanor offenses; traffic cases; civil actions up to $15,000

COUNTY COURTS

Misdemeanor offenses; traffic cases; civil actions up to $15,000

COURT OF CLAIMS

Judges assigned by Supreme Court

All suits against the state for personal injury, property damage, contract and wrongful death; compensation for victims of crime; three-judge panels upon request

MAYOR'S COURTS

Violations of local ordinances and state traffic laws; not courts of record

Source: Supreme Court of Ohio

CHAPTER FIVE

The Executive
Elected Officials

The executive branch of Ohio's state government consists of six elected officials: the governor, lieutenant governor, attorney general, secretary of state, auditor of state, and treasurer of state. All are elected to serve four-year terms, with the governor and lieutenant governor elected on a single ballot as a team. All are limited by the Ohio Constitution to two consecutive terms but may run again after four years out of that office. Elections are held in even-numbered years (2006, 2010, 2014, etc.) between presidential elections. In addition to these six offices, the executive branch includes the departments or agencies responsible for administering state policy in major areas such as finance, transportation, health, human services, and natural resources. These departments and agencies are established by law and may be abolished or altered legislatively. Additional boards and commissions have been established for specific purposes and are also part of the executive branch.

Governor

The governor is the head of the executive branch of state government. It is the governor's responsibility to ensure that all laws are faithfully executed; report the condition of the state to the legislature at each session of the General Assembly; make recommendations to each session of the General Assembly; and, in odd-numbered years, present a proposed state budget for the next biennium.

The governor plays an important role in legislative matters as well. All legislation must be acted upon by the governor, either by signing the act into law or by vetoing the measure. The governor may veto an entire measure passed by the General Assembly, or in the case of appropriation bills, the governor may veto individual items. In either case, a three-fifths vote of each house is required to override the veto. If the bill is not returned to the legislature within ten days, excluding Sundays, it becomes a law as though it had been signed. If the legislature adjourns, making a return to the legislature impossible, the bill becomes a law unless the governor files it along with objections in writing in the Office of the Secretary of State within ten days.

The governor must coordinate all of the agencies in the state's executive branch, oversee preparation of the budget, and supervise state programs.

The Governor's Powers

Compared with other states, Ohio has what is known as "strong" gubernatorial powers. The strength of such power is determined by a governor's appointment powers and veto powers.

The governor exercises wide executive authority beyond that granted in the Ohio Constitution through the power of appointment. With the consent of the Senate, the governor appoints the directors of all administrative departments except the Department of Education. Appointive responsibility extends beyond department or agency heads to many of the heads of divisions within departments and to members of numerous boards and commissions created by the legislature. The governor can create new commissions and boards by executive order. The makeup of the governor's cabinet varies from administration to administration, but it usually includes the department heads and any others whom the governor may invite to sit with them. In 2004, the cabinet consisted of 21 department heads and the lieutenant governor.

The governor represents the state at conferences called by the U.S. President or by other states. Such participation helps define the state's stance on issues of regional or national importance. Conferences may deal with such questions as the control of emissions from power plants, a Midwestern agricultural policy, or economic development.

Lieutenant Governor

The lieutenant governor succeeds to the office of governor in the event of the death, conviction on impeachment, resignation, or disability of the governor. In case of disability, the lieutenant governor serves as governor until the disability ends as determined by the Supreme Court of Ohio. The gubernatorial line of succession extends from lieutenant governor to president of the Senate to speaker of the House of Representatives.

The lieutenant governor is elected jointly with the governor. As with U.S. President and Vice President, a single vote is cast for both candidates in the general election. A constitutional amendment passed in 1989 provides that, in the case of a vacancy in the office of lieutenant governor, the governor nominates a lieutenant governor, who will take office upon confirmation by both houses of the General Assembly.

The lieutenant governor is a member of the governor's cabinet, serves as chief liaison to county and local governments, and has other executive duties as assigned by the governor or as provided by law. The lieutenant governor may be appointed as a department head or as the governor's representative on various boards or commissions.

Attorney General

The chief legal officer of the state is the attorney general and represents the state in all cases in which the state is a party or has a significant interest. The attorney general's office provides legal counsel to all elected state officials, state departments, commissions, and the General Assembly. Most often, this representation is provided through the assignment of an assistant attorney general to work on a regular basis with a given agency. The staff includes more than 300 attorneys.

The attorney general provides formal and informal opinions on Ohio law in response to requests from elected state officials, the General Assembly, the heads of state departments and agencies, and the 88 county prosecutors.

In addition, the attorney general's office enforces Ohio's laws dealing with consumer frauds, antitrust, environmental protection, nursing home patient abuse and neglect, organized crime, and charitable foundations. The attorney general provides direct assistance to Ohio's local law enforcement agencies through the Bureau of Criminal Identification and Investigation. Upon request, the bureau provides investigative services including scientific analysis of crime scenes and evidence.

The Ohio Peace Officer Training Commission, a nine-member board to advise the attorney general, is appointed by the governor with advice and consent of the Senate. It establishes uniform courses of law enforcement training for sheriff and police departments and other peace officers throughout Ohio. It also supervises the Ohio Peace Officer Training Academy.

The attorney general serves as a member of the State Sinking Fund Commission, which administers the sale and redemption of voter-authorized bonds, and the State Board of Deposits.

Auditor of State

The auditor of state is the chief accounting officer for the state of Ohio and is responsible for auditing all public offices in Ohio, including cities and villages, counties and townships, schools and universities, as well as the many departments, agencies, and commissions of state government. Approximately 4,400 audits are performed each year to determine if public funds have been properly accounted for and properly spent. The office conducts special audits to investigate fraud, waste, and abuse.

The state is served by nine regional offices to make regional administrators, district audit managers, and assistant state auditors more accessible to local government officials. Overall, there are more than 700 auditors who serve under the auditor of state.

The Local Government Services Division was established in 1984 to serve as a fiscal advisory group to all governmental agencies and subdivisions. It prescribes accounting practices for local governments and conducts management studies, fiscal emergency analyses, and training workshops for government at all levels.

In 1990, the auditor of state created the Uniform Accounting Network (UAN). The UAN is designed to provide townships with low-cost, computerized financial record-keeping capabilities. The network allows participating townships, villages, and libraries to obtain computer hardware, computer software, and support services from the state for a small monthly fee. More than 1,500 users take advantage of this service.

In addition to auditing responsibilities, the auditor's office writes more than 11 million warrants (checks) annually for the state payroll, public assistance payments, and payments to the state's suppliers of goods and services.

The auditor distributes all state subsidies and taxes collected on behalf of local governments to local political subdivisions. Electronic Funds Transfers (EFT) are used to deposit such funds directly into the local government's bank account.

The auditor sits on various boards and commissions, including the six public employee retirement systems and the Apportionment Board, and is president of the Sinking Fund Commission.

Secretary of State

The secretary of state is the chief elections officer for Ohio, overseeing the administration of all elections in the state to assure compliance with state and federal laws. Ohio law provides for county boards of elections in each county to carry out the election process under the secretary of state's direction. The secretary of state appoints a four-member bipartisan county board of elections from nominations of the county party central committees and supervises the activities of the boards.

The secretary of state prescribes all registration and election forms, prepares regulations and instructions for conducting elections, and issues various voter information pamphlets and brochures.

Under the general corporation law of Ohio, the secretary of state also keeps a file of all articles of incorporation, amendments, mergers, consolidations, and dissolutions of Ohio corporations, and licenses corporations formed outside Ohio that transact business in Ohio. Trade names, trademarks, and marks of ownership are also filed with the office. The office administers the Uniform Commercial Code (UCC) for Ohio, a database of secured loans—those loans in which collateral is put up by the borrower or debtor—approved by the secretary of state.

The secretary of state is the official custodian of all laws passed by the General Assembly and of the journals of both houses. Administrative rules and regulations of all state departments and agencies must be filed with the office. The secretary of state is secretary of the Sinking Fund Commission, is a member of the Apportionment Board, and chairs the Ballot Board.

Treasurer of State

The treasurer of state serves as the state's banker and chief fiscal officer. If the Ohio treasury were a bank, it would be the largest in the state. Its holdings include both cash and investments held for state and custodial funds. Overall, the treasurer's main duties are to collect, invest, and protect state funds.

One of the most important functions of the Ohio treasurer is the collecting and processing of billions of dollars of taxpayers' money each year. The treasurer does not levy taxes and is not responsible for the administration or enforcement of tax laws. Rather, the treasurer sees that taxes are collected and processed by the swiftest and most accurate methods available.

The treasurer's office collects and processes state taxes, licenses, and fees, with the exception of the four following taxes: personal income tax, liquor gallonage tax, horseracing wager tax, and motor transportation tax. These taxes are collected by the respective administrative agencies and deposited in the Ohio treasury.

The treasurer of state also acts as safekeeper of state and custodial funds. The treasurer is the custodian for the investment assets of the five public pension systems, the Industrial Commission, and various other custodial accounts. The pension systems include Public Employees Retirement System, State Teachers Retirement System, School Employees Retirement System, Police and Firemen Disability and Pension Funds, and the Ohio Highway Patrol Retirement System.

The treasurer manages a public funds investment pool for local government subdivisions. The State Treasury Asset Reserve (STAR Ohio) offers participating school districts, cities, counties, or other local governments a profitable, dependable investment alternative.

The treasurer of state serves on other state boards and commissions and is the statutory chair of the three-member State Board of Deposit; other members are the attorney general and auditor. The treasurer is a member of the Sinking Fund Commission and is a member and ex-officio treasurer of the Ohio Public Facilities Commission. This commission administers bond programs funding capital improvements for higher education, mental health, and park facilities.

The treasurer is the sole issuer of bonds for Ohio's voter-authorized Infrastructure Improvements Program, which makes monies available to local governments to fund projects to improve roads, bridges, and other infrastructure activities. The treasurer also issues bonds for the Ohio School Facilities Commission, which provides funding for the construction or renovation of school buildings.

CHAPTER SIX

The Executive
State Government Departments

L aws enacted by the Ohio General Assembly are by and large carried out
by 22 administrative departments in the executive branch. They are, in
the order listed in this chapter:

- the Adjutant General's Department;
- the departments of Administrative Services, Aging, Agriculture, and
  Alcohol and Drug Addiction Services;
- the Office of Budget and Management;
- the departments of Commerce, Development, and Education;
- the Environmental Protection Agency;
- the departments of Health, Insurance, and Job and Family Services;
- the departments of Mental Health, Mental Retardation and Developmental Disabilities, Natural Resources, Public Safety, Rehabilitation and Correction, Taxation, and Transportation;
- the Bureau of Workers' Compensation; and
- the Department of Youth Services.

The governor appoints all department heads with the exception of the
superintendent of public instruction, who is appointed by the State Board of
Education to oversee the Department of Education.

While there is no established pattern for the structure of a department,
most operate through a number of **divisions** or **bureaus** appropriate to
the assigned duties; divisions may be subdivided into *offices*. Usually
division heads are appointed by, and responsible to, the director of the
department; in a few cases, the governor has appointment power. The attorney general represents all state departments in court matters.

State agencies adopt rules of procedure for administering state laws
and must hold public hearings before their adoption. Major *boards* and
commissions relating to each department are included in the descriptions
of departments.

Adjutant General's Department

The Adjutant General is the military chief of staff to the governor and assists and advises the governor in matters affecting the security of the state and the operation of its military forces. The adjutant general is responsible for supervision of military property owned by the state or issued to it by the federal government. The office also maintains military service records.

The adjutant general is responsible for the operation of the **Ohio National Guard**, made up of both army and air units. As of 2004, the total strength was nearly 16,000 officers and enlisted personnel. Each unit has a deployment priority in U.S. Department of Defense war plans.

The **Ohio Military Reserve** is a military force organized and maintained to provide the state with defense in the event the Ohio National Guard is employed or mobilized.

The governor, as commander-in-chief, may order units of the organized forces to provide aid to local civil authorities and areas in the event of damage due to natural disasters such as floods and tornadoes. Through the governor, local civil authorities may request that the Guard come in to protect people and property from looting and/or fire. The National Guard can also be employed to suppress riots, insurrection, and other civil disturbances.

Department of Administrative Services

The Department of Administrative Services (DAS) provides assistance to other state agencies in matters pertaining to personnel, equal opportunity, building construction and renovation, computer information systems, and the procurement of goods and services. There are four divisions of the department.

The **Computer Services Division** delivers computing and telecommunication services to all state government agencies through several operating sections that include the Ohio Data Network, Telecommunications Management, Acquisition Management and the Office of Policy and Planning. The *Ohio Data Network* provides reliable, secure, cost-effective network and mainframe services from its location at the *State of Ohio Computer Center*. *Telecommunications Management* offers telephone, networking, and videoconferencing services and Internet access to schools, libraries, and state agencies. *Acquisition Management* assists state agencies with procuring information technology systems and services by developing and evaluating bid documents and requests for proposals. The *Office of Policy and Planning* administers a long-range technology planning program, coordinates multi-agency initiatives, and issues policies and guidelines for deploying information technology in state government.

The **Equal Opportunity Division** assists state agencies with promoting equal access to state employment and contracting opportunities. This division monitors personnel and business activity. Regarding personnel, the division helps ensure that discrimination does not occur in state agencies or on boards and commissions. To help ensure that minority-owned businesses have access to business opportunities with the state, the division operates the *Historically Underutilized Business* and *Minority Business Enterprise* programs.

The **General Services Division** provides support to all state agencies, including centralized printing, purchasing, motor pool, and mail services. The division administers the federal and state surplus property programs, making surplus property available to eligible agencies or organizations and political subdivisions. In addition, this division is responsible for the control, maintenance, and disposal of state records. It provides and maintains office quarters for the departments, agencies, and commissions of state government. The *State Architect's Office* is responsible for the planning, supervision, and construction of all capital-funded construction improvement projects. *Energy Services* is responsible for reducing energy costs in state government buildings and operations. Some of its duties include reviewing building designs, renovating buildings for energy efficiency, and buying gas and electricity at the lowest prices.

The **Human Resources Division** provides services and information to assist state agencies in carrying out their personnel functions, including payroll and benefits administration, recruitment, policy development, and testing administration. The division oversees training and tuition-assistance programs for state employees. This division also includes the *Office of Collective Bargaining*, which acts as the state's representative in matters pertaining to collective bargaining agreements affecting state agencies, boards, and commissions. The office negotiates and administers labor agreements with six state unions representing 44,000 employees. Such administration includes negotiations, contract compliance, arbitration and grievance processing, research, and training.

Department of Aging

The mission of the Ohio Department of Aging is to serve and represent nearly two million Ohioans age 60 and older. The department's role is to advocate for the needs of all older citizens. The emphasis is on improving the quality of life for older Ohioans, helping senior citizens live active, healthy, and independent lives, and promoting positive attitudes toward aging and older people. The department is committed to helping frail older adults remain at home by providing home- and community-based services when appropriate and feasible in terms of quality and cost.

The Department of Aging channels federal and state funds to 12 regional agencies, which in turn contract with local agencies to provide specific services such as home-delivered meals, transportation, home health aides, and home repair.

One of the most visible programs administered by the department is the Golden Buckeye Card Program for persons 60 years old and older and/or 18 years old or older who are totally and permanently disabled. It provides discounts on products and services from participating merchants statewide. In addition, seniors can use their Golden Buckeye Card for savings on prescriptions at participating pharmacies throughout Ohio. The PASSPORT program provides in-home services to older persons who are Medicaid eligible.

The department has a *Long-Term Care Ombudsman Office* to serve as a mediator and advocate for the rights of older consumers.

Department of Agriculture

The Department of Agriculture enforces state agricultural regulations governing the production, handling, distribution, and marketing of agricultural products. It is also responsible for promoting agricultural development and various state-federal programs benefiting Ohio farmers. Consumer protection activities and regulation of the conduct of county and independent fairs fall within the department's area of the responsibility.

The department's responsibilities are carried out by 12 divisions and programs. The **Animal Industry Division** is responsible for diagnosis and control of diseases affecting livestock and poultry and for veterinary inspection of livestock. The **Division of Food Safety** operates an inspection program to protect the consumer against unclean, adulterated, or mislabeled food, dairy products, beverages, nonprescription drugs, and cosmetics. The **Markets Division** directs domestic and international marketing programs for agricultural products of the state. The **Meat Inspection Division** ensures that meat and poultry products are wholesome, unadulterated, and properly labeled. The **Plant Industry Division** regulates the processing and sale of fertilizers, feed, pesticides, and seeds; it also licenses pesticide applicators and dealers who sell restricted-use pesticides. The division works to control diseases of plants and honey bees, and pests that injure crops.

The division also licenses grain handlers and enforces regulations to protect the grain industry. The **Dairy Division** is responsible for ensuring the safety and wholesomeness of all milk products produced in Ohio. The **Livestock Environmental Permitting Program** regulates the state's largest livestock and poultry farms in areas including construction standards for all new farms; all aspects of manure storage, handling, transportation, and land-application by these farms; and the farms' insect and rodent control plans.

> ## Bungee Jumping . . . and Agriculture
>
> *The Department of Agriculture regulates bungee jumping in the state of Ohio through its Division of Amusement Ride Safety.*

The **Division of Amusement Ride Safety** licenses, inspects, and ensures proper insurance coverage for all temporary and permanent rides in the state of Ohio. The division also conducts re-inspection of rides, investigates accidents, and licenses games at Ohio's numerous county and independent fairs.

The **Enforcement Division** supervises and directs the criminal and administrative investigation programs for the department to determine compliance with federal, state, and local laws in those areas administered by the Department of Agriculture.

The **Division of Weights and Measures** enforces all laws relating to the accuracy of scales and measuring devices to protect the buyer and seller in all commercial transactions. A laboratory at the Department's Reynoldsburg campus provides testing and calibration services to local jurisdictions.

The **Consumer Analytical Laboratory** conducts laboratory tests of food samples and agricultural commodities as required by all divisions.

The **Administration Division** provides support services for the department and maintains a toll-free hot line for consumer questions and complaints about food products, short-weighted packages, package labeling, etc.

Additionally, the Department administers an office of farmland preservation to help with farmland protection efforts. Other programs under the direction of the Department are the Ohio Rural Development Partnership, which addresses the needs of rural Ohio communities; the Ohio Grape Industries Program, which oversees and implements promotional programs for the grape and wine industries; and the Office of Tobacco Programs, which helps develop economic options for Ohio's tobacco farmers and distributes funds from the 1999 National Tobacco Grower Settlement Trust.

Department of Alcohol and Drug Addiction Services

As one of only six states in the nation to address the issue of substance abuse at the cabinet level, the Department of Alcohol and Drug Addiction Services plans, initiates, and coordinates a comprehensive system of alcohol and other drug addiction services designed to prevent abuse and to treat Ohio's addicted populations. The department coordinates its services with other state agencies, the criminal justice system, law enforcement, the legislature, local agencies, and treatment/prevention professionals throughout the state. Working in cooperation with boards at the local level, the department allocates federal and state funds to local Alcohol and Drug Addiction Services/Alcohol, Drug Addiction, and Mental Health Services (ADAS/ADAMH) Boards, which fund local programs for the delivery of community-based services.

The department's programs include: Binge Drinking Prevention; Driver Intervention Programs; Drug Courts; Drug-Free Workplace; Partnership for a Drug-Free Ohio; Preschool Prevention; Prison-Based Therapeutic Communities; Safe and Drug Free Schools and Communities; Treatment Alternatives to Street Crime; Teen Institute; Underage Drinking; Urban Minorities Alcoholism and Drug Abuse Outreach Programs; and Violence Prevention.

Office of Budget and Management

The Office of Budget and Management (OBM) is the staff agency for fiscal matters. It is responsible for preparing the governor's proposed budget and controlling state spending according to law.

The major responsibility of this office is to formulate and execute the budget for the state. Budget requests from state agencies are coordinated with anticipated revenues and with the governor's priorities. The budget, presented to the legislature at the beginning of its first regular session in odd-numbered years, forms the basis for the legislature's appropriation of funds for state programs. Staff members monitor legislative budget hearings and provide program and cost information. After the budget passes, the office schedules spending according to the adopted budget and continually reviews and monitors programs of state agencies as part of the budget control process.

The OBM has responsibility for maintaining the state's financial records and performing pre-audits on invoices.

Department of Commerce

The Department of Commerce's primary task is to regulate state-chartered financial institutions such as banks, savings and loans, credit unions, brokerage houses, and small loan companies. The department licenses and monitors various other commercial activities in order to protect the people served by the industries it regulates. The Department of Commerce recovers its costs through fees and assessments for its services.

The department consists of eight divisions, including the **Division of Administration**, which acts as a service entity to the entire department.

The **Division of Financial Institutions** regulates financial institutions chartered in Ohio. The duties performed by the division include chartering depository institutions, registering and licensing non-depository financial services, and conducting on-site examinations. Industries regulated by this division are banks, savings and loan/savings banks, credit unions, and consumer finance organizations. Consumer finance organizations include check-cashing services, credit service organizations, insurance premium finance companies, mortgage brokers, pawnbrokers, precious metals dealers, second mortgage businesses, and small loan businesses. All examinations, supervision, and regulation activities are performed by division staff who specialize in the operations of each of these specific industries.

The **Division of Industrial Compliance** (DIC) is a diverse regulatory agency that provides building and construction plan reviews; inspections of plumbing, electrical, and structural systems; and on-site inspections of elevators, boilers, and bedding and upholstered products throughout the state. Additionally, the division provides testing, certification, licensing and continuing education services for numerous skilled trades within Ohio's building industry. The division licenses travel agents/tour promoters as well.

The DIC has three bureaus: the *Bureau of Construction Compliance*, the *Bureau of Operations and Maintenance*, and the *Bureau of Licensing and Certification*. The Division of State Fire Marshal's Bureau of Underground Storage Tank Regulations (BUSTR) is housed with DIC.

In addition, DIC provides administrative support for several regulatory and oversight boards that govern policies, procedures, and safety requirements within the construction industry. The *Board of Building Standards* works with federal and state agencies to establish rules governing the erection, construction, repair, alteration, and maintenance of buildings. The *Board of Building Appeals* receives, reviews, and provides findings on construction plan issues, including violations of the Ohio Basic Building Code.

The *Ohio Construction Industry Examining Board* establishes certification requirements for electrical, plumbing and hydraulics, heating, ventilation, air conditioning, and refrigeration contractors as well as overseeing the examination and certification process for these professions. The *Ski-Tramway Board* establishes safety standards and inspection processes for the operation of passenger tramways at ski areas in Ohio.

The **Division of Liquor Control** is responsible for controlling the manufacture, distribution, and sale of all alcoholic beverages in Ohio. The division is the state's sole purchaser and distributor of liquor containing more than 21 percent alcohol by volume. Liquor is sold through more than 415 private businesses that contract with the state to serve as state liquor agencies. Significant sales and tax revenues are generated from the sale of spirituous liquor. These revenues go to the Department of Development for the retirement of economic development bonds; to the Department of Alcohol and Drug Addiction Services for statewide alcohol education, prevention, and treatment programs; to the Department of Public Safety's Liquor Enforcement Division; to the Department of Health's Alcohol Testing Program; and to the *Liquor Control Commission*. Regulatory functions handled by the division include the issuance of permits to the state's approximately 24,000 privately owned and operated manufacturers, distributors, and retailers of alcoholic beverages. The division also regulates industry compliance with the laws pertaining to the manufacture, importation, and distribution of alcoholic beverages containing less than 21 percent alcohol by volume.

The **Division of Real Estate and Professional Licensing** licenses real estate brokers and salespersons, auctioneers, private investigators, and security guards. General and residential appraisers are also licensed and certified. In addition, the division regulates foreign real estate brokers and salespersons, and registers foreign real estate property. Applicants are screened by division staff to assure that legal qualifications for licensure are met. Additional protection is provided to the public by requiring licensees to be bonded. The division is charged with investigating allegations of misconduct and fraud by real estate brokers and salespersons.

The division supports the *Ohio Cemetery Dispute Resolution Committee* by registering all active cemeteries in Ohio and investigating complaints or disputes involving registered cemeteries.

The **Division of Securities** regulates the sale of securities in Ohio by administering the Ohio Securities Act. The act requires the licensing of those who sell securities, provides for the registration of certain types of securities sold, and prohibits certain conduct in connection with the sale of securities. Under the act, the division has responsibility for protecting investors from unfair and fraudulent practices in the securities industry. By administering and enforcing the act, the division promotes an honest and fair securities market in Ohio where individuals and businesses can raise capital and investors can expect a fair return on their investment. Ohio law defines "security" broadly to include stocks, bonds, mutual funds, options, commercial paper, and many other investment opportunities.

The **Division of State Fire Marshal** is responsible for modernizing and enforcing the Ohio Fire Code, designing and presenting fire-prevention programs, analyzing fire-related criminal evidence, investigating the cause and origin of fires and explosions, training firefighters, and regulating underground storage tanks.

The **Division of Unclaimed Funds** regulates the safekeeping and return of monies designated as "unclaimed." Each year more than 100,000 people and organizations lose track of monies, rights to monies, and intangible personal property in Ohio. The division ensures that organizations report unclaimed funds to the state and work to locate the owners of such funds. Common sources of unclaimed funds include dormant bank accounts, unpaid insurance policies, unreturned utility and rent deposits, undelivered and uncashed dividends and shares of stock, uncashed checks, and forgotten layaway deposits.

Department of Development

The Department of Development (DOD) was established to oversee the creation, retention, and expansion of job opportunities in the state of Ohio. DOD works to retain companies already located in Ohio, as well as attract national and international companies to locate their operation in Ohio and provide assistance to Ohio companies looking to export their products to new markets. Other departmental programs assist entrepreneurial and minority business growth, help build healthy communities, and keep the state competitive in world markets. The department is divided into eight divisions and operates 12 regional offices.

The department's regional offices serve as outreach centers that deliver economic development incentives and services to local governments, businesses, professional economic development agencies, and the general public. The regional offices are located in Columbus, Toledo, Lima, Dayton, Cincinnati, Mansfield, Chillicothe, Cleveland, Akron, Cambridge, Marietta, and Youngstown. Each office concentrates on economic development within its region of responsibility. The typical office is headed by a Governor's Regional Economic Development Representative and staffed by other business development specialists to provide prospective companies essential geographic, economic, educational, and industrial information about the region they serve.

The **Economic Development Division** (EDD) provides businesses with assistance ranging from direct financial assistance to small business counseling. Additionally, the division works closely with Ohio's communities to address their needs in terms of economic development. EDD provides financial assistance to companies by providing tax incentives, grants, bonds, and low-interest financing for fixed assets. The division provides technical assistance through funding of Small Business Development Centers and business assistance programs.

Six offices coordinate various parts of the division's responsibilities. The *Office of Business Development* works with Ohio companies, as well as out-of-state companies looking to expand or locate in Ohio. The office structures incentive packages, provides information on Ohio's assistance programs, and conducts searches for these companies. The *Office of Tax Incentives* assists business and local communities to implement Ohio's tax incentive programs. The *Office of Credit and Finance* administers the department's loan programs. The financing programs provide direct loans and bonds for businesses locating or expanding in Ohio that demonstrate they will retain or create jobs. The *Loan and Grant Servicing Office* monitors all existing EDD loans and grants and maintains the document files. The *Office of Workforce Development* provides policy direction and program support on various workforce issues affecting Ohio businesses and offers administrative support to the Governor's Ohio Workforce Policy Board. The board also helps the governor set performance goals and priorities, continuously improves the state's workforce development system, and assists those local leaders who will shape workforce development policy at the local level. The primary programs supported by the office include the Ohio Investment in Training Program (OITP) and other miscellaneous discretionary projects

---

Do You Have Unclaimed Funds?

The Ohio Department of Development's Division of Unclaimed Funds has a Web site so that individuals may check for details of unclaimed funds: http://www.unclaimedfundstreasurehunt.ohio.gov.

funded by federal Workforce Investment Act monies. The primary program of the *Office of Small Business* is the Ohio Small Business Development Center (SBDC) initiative. The office assists with small business creation and growth by providing in-depth business planning and development assistance, including assistance in obtaining necessary business permits.

The **Minority Business Development Division** oversees several offices and programs that assist minority-owned as well as socially and economically disadvantaged business enterprises. These programs include the *EDGE Program* (Encouraging Diversity, Growth, and Equity), the *Minority Contractors and Business Assistance Program,* and the *Procurement Technical Assistance Center Program.* Through these programs the division oversees the delivery of client services including management, technical, financial, and state contract procurement assistance; management analysis; educational services; loans; and bond packaging services. Additionally, the *Procurement Technical Assistance Center* provides assistance to any Ohio business in identification of public sector (federal, state, and municipal) contracting opportunities and bid packaging. The office also assists public sector buyers in locating vendors and suppliers able to provide commodities needed to fulfill bids.

The **International Trade Division** (ITD) promotes exports for Ohio companies and encourages direct foreign investment in Ohio. As part of the export promotion and assistance effort, the division provides companies with current market information and country profiles, advice on market penetration, and contacts with potential business partners in foreign markets. ITD provides trade leads and trade show information and also organizes trade show and business mission delegations. ITD works in conjunction with the state's international trade offices located in Brussels, Belgium; Tokyo, Japan; Hong Kong, China; Toronto, Canada; Tel Aviv, Israel; Mexico City, Mexico; São Paulo, Brazil; and Johannesburg, South Africa. These international trade offices offer assistance to foreign companies seeking Ohio businesses as suppliers of products and services. The offices also serve Ohio companies in need of representation in these markets and those interested in joint ventures, licensing agreements, and technology transfers.

The **Technology Division** is helping to advance Ohio's tradition of innovation through programs designed to provide a sustainable competitive advantage for technology-based businesses within the state. Through strategic partnerships among government, industry, and academia, the Technology Division's coordinated programs focus on four goals: 1) fostering an entrepreneurial climate that accelerates the creation and expansion of high-tech, high-growth businesses in Ohio; 2) ensuring that a complete and effective commercialization infrastructure is in place to capitalize upon major areas of research excellence in Ohio; 3) advancing the global competitive position of manufacturing and technology-based businesses in Ohio; and 4) improving the agility and operational efficiency of the Technology Division to better serve customers and maximize technology-related opportunities.

The **Community Development Division** (CDD) administers a variety of state and federally funded programs that benefit Ohio individuals and families. CDD coordinates its programs to form a comprehensive strategy to build stronger, healthier communities throughout the state. Through partnerships with local governments, community action agencies, other community-based nonprofit service providers, and private-sector funding sources, CDD helps to support local economic development activities to create and retain jobs; rehabilitate communities and neighborhoods through affordable housing and infrastructure improvements; provide weatherization services, energy efficiency incentives, and assistance with home heating bills; provide emergency shelter along with transitional and permanent housing for the homeless; and provide job training and emergency food, shelter, and medical services.

The **Ohio Housing Financing Agency** (OHFA) plays an integral role in the state's housing and community development strategy. OHFA provides financing for the acquisition, construction, and rehabilitation of single-family and multifamily rental housing projects for low- and moderate-income individuals and families. The agency provides low-interest financing to help Ohioans purchase their first homes, as well as distributes housing assistance payments on behalf of low-income tenants in federal housing developments. The OHFA is controlled by a board of directors appointed by the governor. OHFA supports its programs primarily through the issuance, sale, and repayment of bonds, as well as through contract fees.

The Ohio **Division of Travel and Tourism** promotes the Ohio travel and film industries. The division works in partnership with the private-sector travel industry to promote the state as a tourist destination and increase visitor spending in Ohio. The division's six program areas work to increase interest in Ohio tourism through distribution of travel literature, operate the www.DiscoverOhio.com Web site and the toll-free 1-800-BUCK-EYE information line, and generate free and paid publicity.

The **Governor's Office of Appalachia** (GOA) facilitates economic and social development in the 29 Appalachian counties of Ohio. The office, involved with both short- and long-term planning, also serves as an advocate for the region by developing policy and promoting specific projects and proposals that originate from the region's residents.

GOA advises local groups and residents of possible funding sources and methods for addressing problems and acts as a liaison to connect people and resources. GOA also works closely with the Appalachian Task Force, the official citizens advisory group for the region.

GOA receives approximately $4 million annually from the Appalachian Regional Commission (ARC) to administer the state ARC program and fund special project development. GOA coordinates this effort with the three Appalachian Local Development Districts: Buckeye Hills Hocking Valley Regional Development District in Marietta, Ohio Mid-Eastern Governments Association (OMEGA) in Cambridge, and Ohio Valley Regional Development Commission (OVRDC) in Waverly. In addition, GOA receives $4.4 million annually from the state of Ohio for ARC-type grants.

Department of Education

"Religion, morality, and knowledge being necessary to good government and the happiness of mankind, schools and the means of education shall forever be encouraged," stated the ordinance of 1787 that created the Northwest Territory. The Ohio Constitution continued by instructing the General Assembly to "make such provisions by taxation or otherwise, as . . . will secure a thorough and efficient system of common schools throughout the state."

The Ohio Department of Education (ODE) is the government agency responsible for overseeing the system of primary and secondary education in the state of Ohio. Educational services are provided by Ohio's 613 local school districts.

The Department is governed by the **State Board of Education**. The board was created in 1956 to exercise general supervision of public education in Ohio. The board consists of 19 members. Eight are appointed by the governor, and the remaining 11 members are elected by the voters of Ohio. State Board of Education districts are composed of three contiguous Ohio Senate districts. Members are elected on a nonpartisan ballot for six-year terms. The board regulates every school in the state from preschool through high school, both public and private; sets standards for educating and licensing teachers; and makes legislative and budgetary recommendations to the governor and the General Assembly. The Board also appoints a state superintendent of public instruction to administer education policy for Ohio's elementary and secondary students.

STATE BOARD OF EDUCATION DISTRICTS

Courtesy of the Secretary of State's Office

ODE carries out the policies of the State Board of Education under the direction of the superintendent of public instruction. Associate superintendents supervise the five primary centers that carry out the responsibilities of the department. In addition, ODE has created an Office of Field Relations to provide professional development and technical assistance to school districts most in need of improvement.

The **Center for Curriculum and Assessment** is responsible for establishing clear, high standards for each grade level, devising statewide curricula to help local school districts meet these standards, and developing diagnostic and achievement assessments to measure progress and inform instruction. This center also is charged with overseeing the state's involvement in career-technical and adult education.

The **Center for Reform and Urban Education** builds capacity in districts and schools by setting standards, integrating technical assistance, providing professional development, and assessing the results for school districts and buildings. Additionally, the center's responsibilities include the Cleveland Scholarship and Tutoring Program, chartered nonpublic schools, alternative schools, and collaborative reform initiatives such as early college high schools.

The **Center for the Teaching Profession** is responsible for creating educator standards, which define what teachers and principals should know and be able to do at certain points in their careers. Additionally, the center administers state laws governing the licensure of teaching professionals;

Alternative Education in Ohio

The Ohio General Assembly enacted legislation in 1996 and 1997 to create new alternatives in the Ohio education system. In 1996, the Cleveland Scholarship Program established a voucher system that allows eligible students to attend a private school of their choosing. Since its inception, the program has been under judicial review, but has continued.

Another newly introduced alternative is the community or charter school. Ohio's community school laws were passed in 1997, allowing the establishment of publicly funded independent schools that provide a choice in public education. In May 2004, 183 community schools serving more than 48,000 students had opened throughout Ohio, with more expected.

works to ensure that all teaching institutions meet state minimum standards; and handles teacher recruitment and retention, professional development, and rewards and recognitions.

The **Center for School Finance** distributes funds and assists districts with managing fiscal resources.

The **Center for Students, Families, and Communities** provides guidance for reading improvement, early childhood education, exceptional children (disabled/gifted), safety, health, and nutrition. The Ohio School for the Deaf and the Ohio School for the Blind are part of this center.

The **Office of Field Relations** is responsible for professional development and technical assistance to districts, especially those that are low-performing. These services are provided directly by ODE or through a statewide provider system that is coordinated by ODE.

Environmental Protection Agency

The Ohio Environmental Protection Agency (Ohio EPA or OEPA) administers state and federal laws regulating clean air and water, solid waste disposal standards, hazardous materials management, drinking water safety, and cleanup of contamination caused by emergencies or long-term practices. Eight program-based divisions within the agency carry out Ohio EPA activities, with a focus throughout on pollution prevention.

The **Air Pollution Control Division** is responsible for achieving and maintaining clean air quality standards to protect the health of Ohioans. It issues permits-to-install and permits-to-operate for sources that may create air pollution, including fugitive dust, requiring the best available technology to reduce emissions. The division monitors ambient air quality through a statewide network of monitors, oversees auto emission inspection programs, and implements provisions of the federal Clean Air Act.

The **Drinking and Ground Waters Division** regulates public water systems to ensure adequate quantity and safe quality of drinking water, certifies water treatment plant operators, monitors safety of drinking water during temporary incidences of contamination, reviews plans for new water treatment systems, assists communities in development of wellhead protection plans, and oversees regulation of certain types of underground injection wells.

Emergency and Remedial Response handles reports of accidental spills and releases of hazardous substances to the environment, oversees cleanup activities at sites where hazardous waste infiltration occurred in the past, and attempts to recover cleanup costs from responsible parties. It manages a voluntary program aimed at making former industrialized sites, known as "brownfields," usable property.

The state is divided into five districts with an office in each district to supervise Ohio EPA's various environmental programs. A state *Office of Emergency Response* answers environmental emergencies on a 24-hour basis and conducts education and training programs for local fire and police personnel.

The **Environmental Services Division** assists the Ohio EPA, other state and local agencies, and private sector interests with chemical and biological research. The division analyzes environmental samples and provides technical assistance.

The **Environmental and Financial Assistance Division** provides financial and technical assistance regarding preservation and conservation initiatives.

The **Hazardous Waste Management Division** issues permits and licenses to facilities that store, treat, and dispose of hazardous waste. These responsibilities are performed in conjunction with the *Hazardous Waste Facility Board*. This five-member board is responsible for approving new hazardous waste facilities and modifications to existing facilities. Applications for board approval are forwarded from the Ohio Environmental Protection Agency. The board is served by a professional staff that conducts technical reviews of the proposed facility or modifications. This technical review helps form the basis of the board's decision to approve or deny the application. Each application is considered before the public in an open hearing, where concerned parties, including citizens affected by the proposal, can give testimony. The board reviews applications and makes decisions based on certain criteria.

Board members include the directors or their designees from the Department of Natural Resources, Ohio Water Development Authority, and the OEPA, along with two state university employees, appointed by the governor. One of the university employees must be a geologist, and the other must be a chemical engineer. The OEPA representative serves as the board's chair.

The **Solid and Infectious Waste Management Division** regulates solid and infectious waste disposal in Ohio. The division reviews plans for new disposal facilities and issues permits-to-install, works with communities on long-range solid waste planning, and oversees and registers certain generators and transporters of infectious waste. The division also regulates composting operations and runs a scrap tire management program.

The **Surface Water Division** regulates all rivers, lakes, and tributaries throughout the state of Ohio. The division is responsible for conducting state-wide biological quality surveys to support water quality management activities. For example, the division issues sports fish consumption advisories for fish caught in Ohio's numerous bodies of water.

Department of Health

The Ohio Department of Health (ODH) is responsible for ensuring access to affordable, quality health care for all of the state's residents. The department promotes healthful and sanitary living conditions in the state through a variety of means, including developing and enforcing state health laws and standards; providing health planning services, technical assistance, and funding to the state's local health departments; creating cooperative efforts between the public and private sectors in preventing disease, disability, and premature death; and assuring that health providers meet federal and state requirements. ODH is not the direct provider of most health services. Instead, ODH relies on local health departments to implement the policies and standards it has established. The department also administers the appropriation of state funds and federal grants that pay for many of the services provided at the local level. For more information on local health departments, see Chapter 9.

The department is headed by a director of health and a seven-member *Public Health Council.* The council is the primary policy-making body within the department. It adopts, amends, and rescinds rules pertaining to public health. It advises the director of health on matters affecting public health and establishes standards for local boards of health to meet in order to receive state subsidies. The governor appoints the council members for seven-year terms. The members of the council are primarily health professionals; however, one slot is reserved for a member of the general public.

Three major divisions provide most of the regulation and technical support offered by the department. These include Family and Community Health Services, Prevention and Quality Assurance.

The **Division of Family and Community Health Services** works to assure that individuals, families, and children have access to community-based health services. This division is divided into seven bureaus that focus on specific health issues. They are *Nutrition Services, Early Intervention Services, Child and Family Health Services, Oral Health Services, Community Health Services and Systems Development, Health Services Information and Operation Support,* and *Children with Medical*

Handicaps. Each of these bureaus works with the local health departments to implement relevant state standards and provide support for local health care workers.

The **Division of Prevention** strives to maintain a healthy population by monitoring health statistics, promoting safety, and controlling chronic and infectious diseases. The division's six bureaus also work closely with local health departments to implement the state standards. The bureaus include *Infectious Disease Control, Surveillance and Information, Health Promotion and Risk Reduction, Environmental Health and Toxicology, Laboratory,* and *Radiation Protection.*

The **Division of Quality Assurance** ensures that quality standards are maintained in both public and private health delivery systems. This is one area of public health services provided at the state level, not the local level. The division has direct oversight of certain health care facilities, including nursing homes, home health agencies, laboratories, freestanding surgery centers, dialysis centers, in-patient rehabilitation facilities, birth centers, radiation therapy centers, mobile diagnostic imaging centers, and in-hospital maternity units. Additionally, this division handles complaints about services rendered in any of these facilities, as well as services in any licensed or Medicare-certified health care facility. Quality Assurance is also responsible for licensing and certifying facilities that participate in both the Medicare and Medicaid programs. The responsibilities of this division are divided among six bureaus: *Health Care Standards and Quality, Regulatory Compliance, Assessment and Improvement, Diagnostic Safety and Personnel Certification, Information and Operational Support,* and *Provider and Consumer Services.*

Department of Insurance

The Ohio Department of Insurance (ODI) is the sole regulator of the Ohio insurance industry and is charged with protecting the purchasing interests of Ohio citizens. The department is divided into different divisions that work cooperatively to accomplish the goals set by the governor and director and to meet departmental obligations defined by Ohio law.

The **Office of Consumer Services** investigates consumer complaints about all types of insurance, seeking to resolve disputes and to identify possible violations of Ohio law. The *Consumer Advocate's Office* is responsible for providing insurance education and information to the public. The Ohio Senior Health Insurance Information Program (OSHIIP) helps older Ohioans understand and resolve problems with health insurance and Medicare.

The **Office of Investigation and Licensing Services** is responsible for finding and correcting violations of Ohio insurance laws. The office is composed of four key areas. The *Enforcement Division* investigates allegations of unethical conduct and internal insurance fraud committed by agents, companies, and their employees. The *Fraud Division* works to identify and investigate external insurance fraud such as auto theft, arson-for-hire, padded claims, and staged or "paper" accidents. The division refers appropriate cases to local and federal prosecutors. The *Market Conduct Division* audits the nonfinancial operations and performance of domestic (based in Ohio) insurance companies—that is, claims handling, advertising, rate setting, etc. *Licensing* oversees the examination and licensure of all of Ohio's insurance agents to ensure that competent and knowledgeable agents practice within acceptable and appropriate business standards. Licenses must be renewed on an annual basis.

Consumer Hot Line

The Department of Insurance's Office of Consumer Service has a toll-free hot line to answer questions and assist consumers who have insurance questions. The office also provides pamphlets, buying guides, and price comparisons. The number is 1-800-686-1526.

The **Office of Legal Services** reviews all corporate transactions such as stock insurance, mergers, acquisitions, and investments of domestic insurers. Legal Services provides legal research and counsel to the department.

The **Office of Property and Casualty Services** reviews all personal and commercial auto, homeowner, and dwelling insurance along with all commercial fire, general liability, and professional liability insurance, which includes medical malpractice, title, surety, and home warranty rates, rules, and filing forms for insurance companies throughout Ohio.

The **Office of Life and Health Services** reviews the contractual provisions of all life and accident policies to ensure compliance with Ohio law and to certify that policy forms are not deceptive or misleading. The office also reviews premium structure to ensure that rates charged are relative to policy benefits. The *Managed Care Division* is another facet of Life and Health Services. This office is charged with licensing prepaid health care plans such as health maintenance organizations, prepaid dental plans, and health care corporations. Additionally, Managed Care reviews all plan rates, filings, and contracts to ensure compliance with Ohio law. It also investigates and resolves member complaints.

Charged with acting as a financial "watchdog," the **Office of Financial Regulation** has as its primary responsibility the monitoring of the financial solvency of licensed insurance companies doing business in Ohio, ensuring that enough money will be available when consumers file claims.

The **Office of General Services** provides administrative support services for the entire department.

Department of Job and Family Services

The Ohio Department of Job and Family Services (ODJFS) was created in 2000 by a merger of the Ohio Department of Human Services and the Ohio Bureau of Employment Services. Its two major functions are to provide services for Ohio families and services for the Ohio workforce. The department consists of 16 offices and divisions. Most ODJFS programs are state supervised and county administered. Some may be designated to serve areas rather than a single county.

Services for Ohio Families

These services are governed by federal programs under the Social Security Act (SSA) and the Personal Responsibility and Work Opportunity Reconciliation Act (PRWORA), plus a few state programs. They include a wide range of services: financial assistance, food stamps, child support, child care, adoption/kinship/foster care, protective services, and health care. Agencies also provide links to other sources of information for food banks, clothing, shelter, and transportation. PRWORA established the Temporary Assistance for Needy Families (TANF) program, which replaced the long-time SSA program known as Aid to Families with Dependent Children. The emphasis was changed from income assistance to work and self-sufficiency.

The **Office of Family Stability** coordinates programs to assist individuals and families in becoming self-sufficient, including cash assistance, food stamps, and support services. The *Bureau of Child/Adult Protection* coordinates those programs designed to address physical abuse, including adult protective services, child protective services, and family violence prevention services.

Ohio implements TANF through a two-part program known as Ohio Works First (OWF) and Prevention, Retention, and Contingency (PRC). OWF provides income assistance, support services (such as child care), developmental activities, and work opportunities to families. Each participant must cooperate in a plan intended to lead to work and self-sufficiency. While the federal program allows for five years of participation, Ohio limits participation to three years.

PRC provides temporary assistance to families to prevent them from going on welfare, to retain employment, or to provide help in an emergency.

The **Office of Health Plans** implements the state and federal Medicaid program, which provides health care to eligible low-income individuals who do not have money for health insurance or medical services. The office is served by five primary bureaus that provide policy or program support focusing on consumer services, long-term care facilities, alternatives to institutional care, Medicaid managed care, and operations.

The **Office for Children and Families** provides child welfare and child care to children and families. It includes preventive services, adoption and kinship care, child and adult protection, child care services, and foster care or out-of-home placement. The *Bureau of Prevention* is charged with licensing child care facilities in the state, including residential treatment facilities, foster homes, emergency receiving facilities, and group homes.

Medicaid or Medicare?

Medicaid and Medicare are frequently confused. Medicare is a federal insurance program for persons 65 or older regardless of income. Medicaid is an aid program to cover health care costs for low-income or disabled individuals.

The **Office of Child Support** oversees the federally mandated child support program. Under Ohio law, all child and spousal support must pass through the child support system. Services include paternity establishment, establishment and enforcement of child support orders, location of noncustodial parents, collection and distribution of child support payments, and other related matters.

Services for Ohio's Workforce

Passed in 1998, the federal Workforce Investment Act (WIA) created a comprehensive workforce investment system. It superseded the Job Training Partnership Act (JTPA) and Job Corps and incorporated some adult education, rehabilitation, and literacy programs. WIA is intended to help workers access the tools they need to manage their careers, and to help U.S. companies find skilled workers. States are required to coordinate all employment and training programs and to develop "one-stop" centers throughout the state. This has meant a major restructuring of the offices formerly known as "employment services," or "job services offices." No-cost employment and training services are available to all Ohioans. There are, however, targeted groups such as adults, dislocated workers, migrant and seasonal farm workers, veterans, persons with disabilities, and youth. Services are provided for both job seekers and employers. The department is also responsible for Labor Market Information (LMI), which collects and publishes labor force, occupational, and industry data. This information assists the state and the public with short- and long-term planning by providing labor force estimates, affirmative action planning data, and industry employment and earning trends. The department is also charged with ensuring compliance with prevailing wage, state minimum wage, minor labor laws, apprenticeship provisions, and safe workplace guidelines in the public and private sectors as they relate to individuals participating in WIA.

The **Office of Workforce Development** supervises the WIA program throughout the state through the *Governor's Workforce Policy Board* and the local service delivery areas. Services provided to participants at the local level include assessment, counseling, job preparation, and training. The office is also responsible for LMI and the organization and operation of the one-stop system. This system is the entry point for any person seeking employment or training services throughout the state.

The **Office of Unemployment Compensation** is responsible for collecting the Federal Unemployment Tax Act (FUTA) taxes from Ohio employers and for paying unemployment benefits to eligible unemployed individuals. The *Unemployment Compensation Advisory Council* (UCAC) recommends to the director, the Unemployment Compensation Review Commission, the governor, or the General Assembly legislation to ensure a sound and legal unemployment compensation program for Ohio. The UCAC has 12 members: the chairs of the standing committees in the Senate and House to which legislation pertaining to unemployment compensation is customarily referred; two members of the Senate, one from each party, appointed by the president of the Senate; two members of the House, one from each party, appointed by the speaker of the House; three members appointed by the governor to represent the employer community; and three members appointed by the governor to represent employees (labor).

Other programs and services for Ohio's workforce include the following:

- Rapid Response Activity works with employees and employers in the event of a large layoff or plant/business closing;
- Trade Adjustment Assistance provides support to workers harmed by imports or a shift of production as a result of the North American Free Trade Agreement or other trade agreements;
- Job Corps offers work camps for youth to receive training and cash assistance; and

- Tax credits to employers who employ workers in certain targeted groups (persons with disabilities, for example).

ODJFS is supported by offices that serve various administrative and management functions, including business, personnel, fiscal, legislative, management information, and research.

Department of Mental Health

The Ohio Department of Mental Health (ODMH) ensures that mental health care is available in all communities. The Ohio Mental Health Act of 1988 shifted mental health service away from central, state-based control to community-based management.

Community mental health systems are funded, reviewed, and monitored by ODMH through 50 county-level boards. These boards serve as the "local mental health authorities," and they plan, fund, and monitor services provided through nearly 500 not-for-profit community mental health agencies. Each board serves one to five counties and has 18 members appointed to four-year terms. County commissioners appoint two-thirds of the board members, while the other third is appointed by the director of the department. Frequently, mental health boards are combined with alcohol and drug addiction community boards. In that case, the director of the Department of Mental Health appoints only three board members, while the director of the Department of Alcohol and Drug Addiction Services appoints the other three. Counties that have a population exceeding 250,000 may establish a separate community mental health board to further address local needs. Seven counties in Ohio have created such boards.

While more people have received mental health services in outpatient settings, there are six state hospitals operated by ODMH to provide inpatient services. Plans for utilization of state hospitals are submitted to ODMH by the boards, and patients are prescreened in the community prior to admission. Some state hospital employees provide services in community settings through state-operated service programs coordinated by the county boards.

Forensic psychiatric centers located throughout the state are certified and partially funded by the department. These centers evaluate persons referred by criminal courts to determine competence to stand trial or sanity at the time of an offense. Two state hospitals operate maximum-security forensic units for persons committed by criminal courts. ODMH also provides mental health services to the Department of Rehabilitation and Correction and to the Department of Youth Services.

Under the department's **Division of Administrative Services**, the *Office of Program Evaluation and Research* evaluates state mental health programs and policy initiatives, develops guidelines for evaluation of community mental health boards, and administers the development and funding of major statewide research projects that examine the mental health needs of Ohio's citizens and the effectiveness of existing programs. The *Office of Education and Training* provides a broad range of programs to increase the skills, knowledge, and abilities of persons who deliver mental health services throughout Ohio. This includes clinical and administrative training mandated by state and federal statute, by ODMH, or by federal grant requirements.

In the **Program and Policy Development Division**, vocational training and jobs programs are provided through the *Office of Jobs and Education* for consumers of mental health services in state hospitals and community settings. This office also works with mental health boards and agencies to advise consumers of employment opportunities in local mental health systems. The *Office of Consumer Services* provides oversight and assistance to programs that support severely mentally disabled persons in the community. The office reviews local mental health systems to ensure that essential services such as mental health care; case management; vocational, educational, and employment programs; housing; and social supports are available to this population.

The *Office of Children Services and Prevention* reviews existing services to children and adolescents, providing direction to local systems to enhance mental health service delivery and availability. The office administers statewide efforts to prevent mental illness and serves as a clearinghouse for information about mental illness and maintaining mental health.

Through its **Division of Support Services**, ODMH provides pharmacy and laboratory services and wholesale food distribution to state hospitals, community mental health agencies, and other state agencies that operate institutions. This office also provides centralized laundry services to state hospitals and developmental centers.

Department of Mental Retardation and Developmental Disabilities

The Ohio Department of Mental Retardation and Developmental Disabilities (MR/DD) ensures the availability of programs, services, and supports for individuals with mental retardation and/or other developmental disabilities. The department works to promote their health and safety and to assist and support the families of these individuals in achieving these goals.

A developmental disability is a severe, chronic disability that is attributed to a mental or physical impairment manifested before the age of 22, is expected to continue indefinitely, and results in substantial functional limitations in three or more areas of major life activities. Examples include cerebral palsy, spina bifida, and mental retardation.

The department is organized under ten divisions: **Audits**, **Community Services**, **Constituent Services**, **Fiscal Administration**, **Medicaid Policy**, **Human Resources**, **Information Systems**, **Legal Services**, **State Operated Services and Supports**, and **Administration**. More than 60,000 Ohioans receive support through the MR/DD system. ODMR/DD distributes resources and funding to the 88 county boards of MR/DD who then administer programs at the local level. The department regulates and provides technical assistance to the boards to ensure quality services.

The department operates 12 developmental centers that provide residential and rehabilitation programs to approximately 2,000 residents. The department provides a wide range of programs and services in the community through the county board system. Each board is composed of seven members, four of whom are appointed by the probate judge of the county. At least two members are parents of individuals eligible for, and currently receiving, services by the county boards of MR/DD. County boards provide services to a wide age span of persons: early intervention (ages 0-2), preschool (ages 3-5), school age (ages 6-21), and adult (ages 16 and up). Among the many services offered are family resource services, supported home services, case management services, transportation services, and community employment services.

Ohio Department of Natural Resources

Created in 1949, the Ohio Department of Natural Resources (ODNR) owns or manages more than 590,000 acres of land for public recreation and the appreciation of nature, including 74 state parks, 20 state forests, 127 nature preserves, 20 state scenic rivers, and 120 state wildlife areas across Ohio. ODNR also has jurisdiction over more than 120,000 acres of inland waters and 7,000 miles of streams, as well as Ohio's portions of Lake Erie and the Ohio River.

Among its other responsibilities, the department regulates oil, gas, and mineral industries in Ohio; manages fish and wildlife resources; maps and defines the state's geologic framework; and promotes recreational boating and enforces boating safety laws. ODNR professionals also manage the state's water resources and its historic canal systems, coordinate activities of county soil and water conservation districts, support local recycling and litter-prevention programs, and oversee the Ohio Coastal Management Program.

There are 12 primary divisions within the Ohio Department of Natural Resources. The **Division of Engineering** provides a full range of engineering and construction services to ODNR's landholding divisions. The **Division of Forestry** manages 20 state forests and provides forest management assistance to private woodland owners in Ohio. The division provides assistance to local communities through urban forestry programs and works to prevent the destruction of forest lands by fires, insects, and disease. The **Division of Geological Survey** studies and publishes information about the mineral resources, fossil fuels, economic geology, geomorphology, stratigraphy, paleontology, mineralogy, and geologic structure of Ohio. ODNR biologists conduct special studies on energy or mineral resources within the state, develop and distribute maps, and produce data portraying Ohio's geology.

The **Division of Mineral Resources Management** regulates oil and gas production, surface and underground mining of coal and industrial minerals, and reclamation activities. It plugs abandoned oil and gas wells and restores abandoned mine lands, enforces mining safety laws, ensures protection of freshwater resources, and maintains a database of oil and gas well owners.

The **Division of Natural Areas and Preserves** manages 127 state nature preserves which represent characteristic examples of Ohio's natural landscape types, natural vegetation, habitat for rare and endangered species, and geological formations. The division oversees a system of 20 state scenic rivers, including three with national scenic river status, that are preserved and protected for the enjoyment of all Ohioans.

Ohio's 74 state parks are overseen by the **Division of Parks and Recreation**. They offer a variety of facilities including resort lodges, cabins, beaches, golf courses, campgrounds, and hiking trails. The **Division of Real Estate and Land Management** provides department-wide planning, environmental-review coordination, and real estate functions as well as the administration of grant programs, including NatureWorks and Clean Ohio Trails Fund. The division is responsible for capital improve-

Wildlife Tax Check-off

Since 1983, citizens have been able to check off a box on their state income tax returns to make donations from their tax refunds to the Natural Areas and Preserve program and to the Non-Game and Endangered Species program.

ment planning through the Statewide Comprehensive Outdoor Recreation Plan (SCORP), canal lands management, administration of the Lake Erie Access Program, and oversight of the coastal management program.

The **Division of Recycling and Litter Prevention** assists in the implementation of Ohio's Solid Waste Management Plan, encouraging Ohioans to recycle waste materials and purchase recycled-content products. More than 70 percent of the division's budget is passed directly to local communities for use in recycling and litter prevention programs. The division coordinates the statewide "Recycle, Ohio!" program and works to stimulate the market for recycled-content products in Ohio. The **Division of Soil and Water Conservation**, working through Ohio's 88 soil and water conservation districts, assists government agencies, businesses, and private landowners in natural resource management and land use planning decisions. It conducts soil inventories and publishes interpretive soil reports and maps, monitors changes in land use, and recommends management practices to meet water quality standards relating to agricultural pollution and urban sediment abatement. The **Division of Water** has broad responsibilities for managing water resources, collecting data, developing groundwater resource and pollution potential maps, and providing technical assistance on ground water quantity management in Ohio. The division issues permits for the construction of dams and inspects existing dams. The division studies all factors relating to flooding and water supply in the state. The **Division of Watercraft** administers and enforces all laws regarding identification, numbering, titling, use, and operation of recreational boats on Ohio's waters; conducts watercraft safety education programs; and develops boating facilities on major water areas of the state. The **Division of Wildlife** promotes hunting and fishing opportunities in the state while it protects and improves wildlife resources, including fish, game, and non-game species through law enforcement, research programs, improvement of habitat, and establishment of native species.

To assist the work of these divisions, there are several centralized support offices within the Department of Natural Resources: *Office of Human Resources, Office of Information Technology, Office of Budget and Finance,* and *Office of Communications.* A number of advisory councils, boards, and commissions have been established to provide public participation in the formulation of plans and policies for the department and its various divisions.

The department was preparing to restructure in late 2004.

Department of Public Safety

The Department of Public Safety promotes safety on Ohio's roads as well as development and implementation of Ohio's Highway Safety Plan. The **Administration Division** compiles, analyzes, and publishes statistics on motor vehicle accidents. It also conducts research and provides materials and programs promoting highway safety. The *Office of the Governor's Highway Safety Representative* is responsible for receiving and allocating federal highway safety monies. This office monitors the local recipients of these funds and determines the allocations based on criteria established by state and federal government.

The **Ohio State Highway Patrol** enforces traffic laws, investigates accidents, assists motorists in distress, and promotes traffic safety. The patrol inspects school and church buses, supervises driver's license examinations, and licenses commercial driving schools and instructors.

The patrol has a telecommunications system, LEADS (Law Enforcement Automated Data System), which connects highway patrol posts, local police, and sheriff's departments with a computer bank containing information on vehicle registration, driver's licenses, outstanding warrants, and "wanted" files. LEADS also connects with the National Crime Information Center in Washington, D.C., and the other states.

The patrol enforces laws on state-owned or leased property and assigns available specially trained investigators to cases that require in-depth investigation. The general headquarters of the patrol is located in Columbus, with 58 patrol posts throughout the state. The director of the Department of Public Safety appoints the superintendent of the State Highway Patrol.

The **Investigative Unit** houses the *Liquor Enforcement* and *Food Stamp Fraud* sections. The Liquor Enforcement section investigates complaints on liquor establishments and enforces underage drinking laws. The Food Stamp Fraud unit investigates complaints against retail establishments and individuals who violate state food stamp law.

The **Bureau of Motor Vehicles** (BMV) issues motor vehicle license plates and registrations, driver's licenses, identification cards, and motor vehicle dealer and salesperson's licenses. BMV is the repository of motor vehicle title records. The registrar of the bureau is appointed by, and serves under, the director of the Department of Public Safety.

Registrations are issued through a statewide network of deputy registrars. Multi-year license plates are issued, with validation stickers issued in off-years. Fees collected for motor vehicle registration are redistributed to local governments, according to a formula set by law, and may be used by them for road construction and repair. Special license plates are issued by the BMV. Extra fees for these license plates are collected and help support specific state entities such as Lake Erie, recreational parks, and wildlife programs.

> ## Motor Voter
>
> *When you visit a deputy registrar of the Bureau of Motor Vehicles to register a vehicle or to change your driver's license because you have moved or changed your name, you may register to vote or update your voter registration at the same time.*

The **Division of Emergency Medical Services** (EMS) is responsible for certifying all emergency medical technicians (EMTs) and fire personnel in the state. It accredits and charters schools for EMT and fire training, and it offers grant monies to EMS organizations for training and equipment. The division also oversees the Emergency Medical Services for Children, a program that focuses on safety issues for children.

The **Ohio Emergency Management Agency** (EMA) is under the umbrella of the Department of Public Safety. EMA is the central point of coordination within the state for response and recovery to disasters. When not in a response or recovery mode, EMA works to ensure that the state and its citizens are prepared to respond to an emergency or disaster. EMA works in conjunction with the 88 county emergency management agencies to respond to emergencies. When an emergency exceeds the capacity of local government, requests for assistance are directed to EMA. If an emergency exceeds the resources of EMA, the state requests assistance from the Federal Emergency Management Agency (FEMA).

The **Ohio Office of Homeland Security**, in conjunction with the State of Ohio Security Task Force, is responsible for coordination of the homeland security efforts and those initiatives of the Department of Public Safety. This office is responsible for allocating homeland security funds to various first-responder and law enforcement agencies throughout the state. The task force consists of 21 representatives of various communications divisions from executive agencies. The task force is chaired by the director of public safety. The task force's mission is to develop a coordinated, integrated, comprehensive state strategy to address security issues by strengthening state preparedness at all levels of government.

There are four working groups under the office: First Responders, homeland security funding, public information, and Citizen Corps.

Department of Rehabilitation and Correction

The Department of Rehabilitation and Correction (DRC) administers and operates Ohio's adult correctional system and provides for the custody and rehabilitation of convicted adult criminal offenders. All adults convicted of felonies for which the sentence is at least six months come into the state's prison system. The department is responsible for the administration and operation of both the institutional and the community-related phases of the adult correctional system, including parole and probation. There are two major functional divisions in the department.

The **Office of Prisons** oversees Ohio's 31 minimum-, medium-, close-, and maximum-security prisons for male and female offenders. The prisons are grouped into two regions for administrative purposes, one north and the other south. A deputy director supervises prison operations in each region and functions as the administrative supervisor for the individual wardens. In addition to providing oversight for prison operations, the Office of Prisons provides support services for all Ohio prisons in the areas of education, classification, critical incident management, recreation, unit management, security, youthful offender programming, and the management of disruptive inmate groups.

The **Division of Parole and Community Services** works in conjunction with local criminal justice officials and community and state agencies to provide community sanctions for adult offenders. Parole, or post-release control, is a period of supervision prior to full release from the state's correctional system. There are three major branches of this division, the *Bureau of Adult Detention*, the *Bureau of Community Sanctions*, and the *Adult Parole Authority*, which includes the *Ohio Parole Board*. The *Office of Victim Services* is also under this division.

The department's **Administrative Division** manages major functions and responsibilities of the department. Major offices include *Administration*, which oversees day-to-day operations and heads up the *Ohio Penal Industries*, which provides industrial training opportunities to Ohio inmates. The *Office of Correctional Health Care* provides inmates with medical services, including mental health and drug/alcohol treatment. The *Office of the Chief Inspector* monitors inmate grievance procedures, assists institutions in attaining accreditation, provides technical assistance in the area of security threat groups, and conducts internal management audits of the department.

DRC works with the *Community Justice Cabinet*, which provides leadership to stimulate change that will achieve a balanced approach to justice practices. The cabinet appoints five councils that review their respective areas of operation and identify ways in which their philosophy of community justice can be incorporated into current practices. Members on the council are DRC staff members, along with professionals from other areas of the justice system.

Department of Taxation

The Department of Taxation has administrative and enforcement responsibilities in most areas of state taxation and in specified areas of local taxation. The department makes rules and regulations for tax administration, prepares reporting forms, collects certain taxes, audits returns, levies tax penalties, and supervises the valuation of real property. The head of the department, called the tax commissioner, appoints division administrators. Eleven operating divisions have jurisdiction over specific taxes or groups of taxes.

The **Sales and Use Tax Division** receives and processes state sales taxes collected by vendors, and collects and distributes local permissive sales taxes for taxing districts that have adopted a local sales tax. The **Excise and Motor Fuel Tax Division** administers the motor fuel (gasoline) and excise taxes, as well as the horse racing taxes and severance taxes. Severance tax is levied on certain natural resources extracted from the soil and water in Ohio. Excise taxes include both cigarette and alcoholic beverage taxes.

The **Personal Income Auditing**, **Corporate Auditing**, and **Income Tax Services** divisions are responsible for administering and processing the personal income, withholding, and corporate franchise taxes.

The **School District Income Tax Division** is responsible for administering this tax, which is imposed on the incomes of residents and on estates in certain school districts who have voted for this source of funding.

The **Taxpayer Services and Compliance Division** oversees services for taxpayers including registration, compliance, and general tax information. This division maintains the Energy Credits Program that reduces the winter heating bills of qualified individuals.

The **Personal Property Tax Division** administers tangible personal property business taxes and the tax on dealers in intangibles. The **Public Utility Tax Division** is responsible for the assessment of all public utility property values and the administration of the public utility excise tax, which is levied on companies classified by statute as public utilities.

The **Tax Equalization Division** is responsible for supervising the valuation of real property by county auditors. The division works to ensure that all real property is taxed uniformly throughout the state as required by the Ohio Constitution and court decisions. It conducts continuous sales ratio studies of real property sales to aid in its determination of uniform appraisals. The division also processes applications for exemption of real property from taxes. The **Estate Tax Division** is responsible for Ohio's inheritance and estate taxes.

The *Tax Commissioner's Hearing Board* reviews taxpayer complaints, assessments, or audits. Appeals from determinations made by the commissioner's board may be made to the *Board of Tax Appeals*, a quasi-judicial board composed of three members appointed by the governor. It hears appeals of decisions of county budget commissions and boards of revision, in addition to those of the tax commissioner.

Department of Transportation

The Ohio Department of Transportation (ODOT) is responsible for planning, building, and maintaining a safe, efficient, and accessible transportation system that integrates highway, rail, and air networks to foster economic growth and personal travel.

The department interacts with local and federal government entities to coordinate the funding of maintenance and new construction projects and to provide technical and administrative assistance. ODOT has direct responsibility for all of Ohio's interstate highways, as well as all U.S. and state routes located outside municipal boundaries. While ODOT-maintained highways account for about 13 percent of the total roadway mileage in the state, they carry 50 percent of the daily traffic. The remaining highways, bridges, and streets are the responsibility of municipalities, counties, and townships.

> ## Real-time Traffic Information
>
> *The Ohio Department of Transportation (ODOT) offers real-time traffic and weather information for citizens from a vast network of pavement sensors, traffic cameras, and weather stations for the state of Ohio at http://www.buckeyetraffic.org.*

New highway construction is financed by state and federal gasoline taxes, with the federal government paying 90 percent of the construction costs of interstate highways and 80 percent of the construction costs of primary and secondary roads. No federal money is used for maintenance. Four subdivisions—state, county, township, and municipality—are each assigned jurisdiction over a specific portion of the highway network. Although the state does not have administrative control over the county, township, and municipal agencies concerned with highways, state law gives the director of ODOT power to coordinate their efforts.

Five offices are located under the director on the department's table of organization: Chief of Staff, Chief Legal Counsel, Highway Management, Planning and Production, and the Division of Information Technology.

Highway Management provides a liaison between the agency's central office and its 12 district offices, providing guidance and supervision for the implementation of policies and procedures. The district offices are responsible for highway management, planning and programs, and production.

Planning and Production comprises four divisions: Planning, Local Programs, Project Management, and Finance and Forecasting. This office is responsible for quality assurance, policy development, and guidance to enable the agency's district offices to make decisions and continue to interject state-of-the-art concepts into all aspects of ODOT's functions.

In addition to the agency's highway responsibilities, ODOT's *Office of Public Transportation* assists local communities with developing, implementing, improving, and funding public transit systems. The *Office of Aviation* works with airports to meet national safety standards, coordinates with the Federal Aviation Administration on all aviation matters related to Ohio's county airport system, provides air transportation to state officials, and maintains the state's aircraft fleet.

The *Transportation Review Advisory Council* was established in 1997 to provide a fair, open and equitable selection process for state funding of major new construction projects. It consists of nine members, including the director of ODOT, who serves as chairperson. Six members are appointed by the governor and one each by the speaker of the Ohio House of Representatives and the president of the Ohio Senate. Members have overlapping terms.

The *Ohio Rail Development Commission*, an independent agency within ODOT, promotes economic development and rail-highway safety.

The five-member *Ohio Turnpike Commission* is the organization that administered the construction and continues the maintenance of the east-west turnpike across the northern part of the state.

Bureau of Workers' Compensation

The Ohio Bureau of Workers' Compensation (BWC) provides medical and wage loss compensation to injured workers or their families for work-related injuries, diseases, or death. The structure of this program is outlined in the Ohio Constitution in provisions adopted in 1912. Responsibility for implementing the program lies with BWC and with the *Industrial Commission of Ohio* (IC). BWC acts as the administrative and insurance arm, while the IC hears and decides contested workers' compensation claims and issues. BWC has a central office in Columbus and 16 regional offices throughout the state.

BWC provides insurance to about two-thirds of Ohio's work force. The remaining workers receive coverage directly through their employers. These companies are part of a self-insurance program for large and financially stable employers that meet strict qualifications set by BWC. In fiscal year 2003, BWC provided workers' compensation coverage to more than 280,000 employers, processed more than 230,000 new claims, and paid out nearly $2 billion in benefits. Premiums and assessments from employers totaled more than $2.1 billion. All BWC premiums are the sole responsibility of the employer and are not passed on to the employee. Premiums are deposited into the State Insurance Fund to cover current and anticipated costs of claims.

The IC is the claims adjudicative arm of Ohio's workers' compensation system. The commission's role is to assist in fairly resolving disputes over the awarding of workers' compensation benefits. Hearings on disputed claims are conducted at three levels within the commission: the district hearing level, the staff hearing level, and the commissioner level. In total, the commission conducts approximately 185,000 hearings each year.

There are three commissioners appointed by the governor. One member represents employers, one employees, and one the public. The governor also selects the chairperson.

In addition to the commissioners, IC hearing officers and members of regional boards of review conduct hearings throughout Ohio for the convenience of all parties. The boards of review act as appellate bodies for appeals of district-level hearings. There are three members of each regional board of review. The boards are bipartisan, and members are appointed by the governor. Each commissioner and each member of a regional board is appointed to a six-year term.

The *Workers' Compensation Oversight Commission* serves as an advisory board to BWC. The commission is responsible for reviewing BWC's investments and investment policy. BWC also seeks advice and consent from the commission in regard to administrative rules. The commission consists of five voting members, representing BWC constituent groups, and four non-voting legislative members. The voting members are recommended to the governor by a nominating committee, and their appointments are confirmed by the Senate. They serve five-year terms and may not be reappointed to more than two full terms. The voting members represent state-funded employers, employees, organized labor, the public, and self-insuring employers. The nonvoting legislators include the ranking minority and majority members of the legislative committees that oversee workers' compensation legislation.

Department of Youth Services

The Department of Youth Services (DYS) is the agency charged with the responsibility for youth between the ages of ten and 21 years who have committed felony offenses and have been committed to institutional care by the juvenile courts. Ohio law permits only felony offenders to be committed to the Ohio Department of Youth Services; youth who commit misdemeanors are assigned to community-based programs by the local county juvenile court. Youth are sent from the juvenile court system to DYS under court-specified minimum sentences based on the degree of seriousness of the offense. Youth committed to DYS must serve at least the minimum sentence unless the committing court approves an early release. After the minimum sentence has been served, the department may retain jurisdiction until the youth reaches the age of 21 or until the department recommends discharge. In cases of murder or homicide, youth must remain with the department until they are 21.

DYS is responsible for the operation of seven facilities, including high- and medium-security facilities for male and female offenders.

DYS operates fully accredited high schools in each facility and also provides the opportunity for young people to earn a GED. In some cases, youth take college correspondence courses that may be applied to a degree at a later date. A vocational education program within each facility teaches welding, barbering, automotive repair, electronics, computers, and similar vocational subjects. Substance abuse and mental health counseling programs are part of the department's programs.

The department has six regional parole offices staffed by personnel who supervise and work closely with any young person released from a DYS facility. Research, data processing, business, personnel, and other essential services are provided by a support staff at the DYS central office.

CHAPTER SEVEN

The Executive
Supplemental Agencies

The smooth operation of state government relies on a variety of "other" executive organizations. These boards, commissions, authorities, and councils provide services focused on particular issues that often cannot be addressed by larger government departments. Supplemental agencies often have minimal staffing and may not function on a daily basis. Funding for each agency is dependent on how the organization was established.

Supplemental agencies can be created by the governor, the legislature, or major departments to advise the departments of state government. While the governor may appoint members to boards and commissions, the balance of powers requires that the Senate consent to the governor's appointments. Many of these supplementary agencies have been included in the discussion of the state departments to which they are related. Others of a more general nature are treated separately here.

Air Quality Development Authority

The Ohio Air Quality Development Authority (OAQDA), created in 1972, contributes to cleaner air in Ohio by assisting Ohio businesses in meeting environmental mandates through financing for the purchase, construction, and/or installation of air pollution control equipment.

OAQDA raises funds through its authority to issue air quality revenue bonds and make loans and grants. OAQDA finances grants to governmental agencies for the acquisition and construction of air quality facilities, and makes loans for air quality projects for industry, commerce, distribution, or research. OAQDA also provides free confidential consultation to companies with fewer than 100 employees through the Clean Air Resource Center.

In July 2003 the General Assembly transferred the Ohio Coal Development Office (OCDO) from the Ohio Department of Development to the Air Quality Development Authority. The repositioning of this agency allows the OAQDA through the OCDO to promote the benefits of clean coal as a source of energy. According to the United States Environmental Protection Agency,

Ohio is the fourth largest consumer of electricity. A majority of Ohio's electricity is generated by burning coal.

Five members of the OAQDA are appointed by the governor. The directors of the Department of Health and the Ohio Environmental Protection Agency serve as well.

Ohio Arts Council

The Ohio Arts Council (OAC), established as a state agency in 1965, encourages, supports, and promotes the arts in Ohio. With funds from the Ohio legislature and the National Endowment for the Arts, the council provides financial assistance to artists and arts organizations. The Ohio Arts Council believes that the arts should be shared by the people of Ohio. The arts arise from public, individual, and organizational efforts. Through the council's five divisions—**Services for Artists**, **Support for Organizations**, **Arts for Communities**, **Arts Partners**, and **Regional Assistance**—the OAC supports and encourages these efforts.

The OAC is composed of 15 voting members appointed to five-year terms by the governor and four nonvoting members, two each from the Ohio Senate and House. The council is the sole body empowered to make final grant decisions. The executive director and OAC staff assist artists and arts organizations by guiding them through the application process and by working with panel consultants to arrive at the funding recommendations presented to council. The council receives a biennial appropriation from the Ohio General Assembly, plus funding received annually through the grants process from the National Endowment for the Arts.

Arts and Sports Facilities Commission

The Ohio Arts and Sports Facilities Commission evaluates the need for Ohio arts and sports facilities and administers their quality planning, design, construction, and operations through cooperation with local nonprofit and government sponsors and the appropriate state agencies. Since 1990, the commission has appropriated more than $390 million dollars to more than 150 projects throughout Ohio.

Created in 1988 by the General Assembly, the commission consists of five voting members appointed by the governor and three *ex-officio* members: the director of the Ohio Arts Council and two members of the Ohio General Assembly, one each appointed from the Ohio Senate and Ohio House of Representatives. The commission reports to the governor and General Assembly.

Ohio Athletic Commission

The Ohio Athletic Commission was created in 1997 by the General Assembly to replace the Ohio Boxing Commission. The purpose of this organization is to regulate professional prize fighting in Ohio. It is made up of five voting members appointed by the governor and two nonvoting members, one of whom is a member of the Ohio Senate and one a member of the Ohio House. The commission prescribes boxing, "tough-man"/"tough-woman," and wrestling rules; issues permits; and licenses promoters and participants. A five percent tax is imposed on the gross proceeds from ticket sales for boxing matches and "tough-man"/"tough-woman" events. The revenue generated goes into the General Revenue Fund.

Ohio Building Authority

The Ohio Building Authority (OBA) was created by the Ohio General Assembly in 1963. Its powers and duties include the authorization to acquire, purchase, construct, reconstruct, equip, furnish, improve, alter, enlarge, maintain, repair, and operate office buildings and related storage and parking facilities for use by departments and agencies of Ohio, as well as local federal agencies in certain circumstances. OBA issues bonds to finance the cost of its projects. In addition, OBA has been given the power to finance the construction of new correctional and transportation facilities and to improve existing structures. OBA consists of five members appointed by the governor for six-year terms.

Ohio Civil Rights Commission

The Ohio Civil Rights Commission (OCRC) is primarily responsible for enforcing the state and federal laws prohibiting discrimination. OCRC receives and investigates charges of discrimination in employment, public accommodations, housing, higher education, and credit.

Discrimination based on race, color, religion, sex, national origin, ancestry, handicap, age, or familial status (families with children) is prohibited. The commission has authority to initiate investigations of discriminatory practices, formulate policies, make periodic surveys of the existence and effect of discrimination, and receive affirmative action progress reports from state and local governments and their subdivisions for preparation of an annual summary report for the Ohio General Assembly. OCRC also prepares a comprehensive antidiscrimination education program for Ohio's public school students.

Any person living or working in Ohio can file a charge of discrimination with one of the commission's regional offices in Akron, Cincinnati, Cleveland, Columbus, Dayton, or Toledo. Charges may be filed by persons aware of alleged discriminatory practices or by individuals who believe they have been discriminated against. The regional offices receive and investigate charges of discrimination and make recommendations. There is no fee for using OCRC services.

The commission consists of a five-member board of commissioners who are the final arbiters in OCRC's internal process. Commissioners are appointed to staggered five-year terms by the governor. They meet regularly to rule on recommendations from staff. Commissioners also appoint the executive director, who implements the policies and rulings of the commission.

Both parties of a discrimination complaint may appeal commission rulings internally to the commission. They also may appeal to the court of common pleas.

The commission is responsible for the oversight and coordination of activities related to the 41-member *Commission on African-American Males*. The members are appointed by the governor to research and recommend strategies concerning social, economic, and educational issues affecting Ohio's African-American male population.

Ohio Community Service Council

In 1994, the General Assembly established the Ohio Community Service Council to administer grants in the state of Ohio under the federal National and Community Service Trust Act of 1993. The agency's original name was the Governor's Community Service Commission. .

The council is responsible for administering AmeriCorps funds in Ohio and for promoting volunteerism and community service through activities such as Make A Difference Day Ohio. The council also oversees Ohio Citizen Corps, a comprehensive effort to engage volunteers in homeland security activities.

The council is composed of 21 members, 13 of whom are appointed by the governor and eight of whom are representatives of state agencies and the Ohio House and Senate. The council is supported by a staff of 15 employees.

Ohio Consumers' Counsel

Established in 1976, the Ohio Consumers' Counsel (OCC) serves as the legal representative for residential utility consumers of Ohio's investor-owned natural gas, electric, telephone, and water companies. The OCC represents consumers in cases before the Public Utilities Commission of Ohio (PUCO), the Ohio Supreme Court, and federal regulatory agencies and courts. The OCC provides a hot line for consumers to discuss problems or complaints with investor-owned utility services and provides materials to educate consumers on utility matters. The compliance section of the OCC protects the interests of residential utility consumers by monitoring and enforcing utility company compliance with regulations, state laws, codes, company rules and regulations. The Ohio Consumers' Counsel has four major departments: Administration, Advocacy Services, Analytical Services, and Communications.

Utility Questions?

Ohio residents may contact the Ohio Consumers' Counsel with questions about utilities at 1-877-PICK-OCC from 8:30 a.m. to 5:30 p.m. or online at http://www.pickocc.org. Ohio residents may also sign up for consumer alert e-mails through the Ohio Consumers' Counsel Web site.

OCC directs the day-to-day operations of the agency with guidance from a nine-member bipartisan governing board, the members of which represent organized labor, family farmers, and at-large residential consumers. The governing board is appointed by the Ohio attorney general.

Commission on Dispute Resolution and Conflict Management

Established in 1989, the Commission on Dispute Resolution and Conflict Management provides dispute resolution and conflict management training, consultation, and technical assistance in designing dispute resolution programs. Facilitation and mediation services are also available. Training is focused on four program areas: educational institutions, state and local government, courts, and communities.

One-third of the 12-member board is appointed by the governor, one-third is appointed by the chief justice of the Supreme Court, and the remaining four are appointed by the president of the Senate and the speaker of the House.

Ohio Educational Telecommunications Network Commission

The Ohio Educational Telecommunications Network Commission (OET) was established in 1961 to foster the orderly growth of public telecommunications in the state. OET's network includes Ohio's 12 public television stations, 33 public radio stations, and nine radio reading services in a statewide system. OET also maintains a relationship with eight education technology departments and foundations. These organizations provide public television stations with instructional programming available to every school in Ohio. In addition to programming services, OET administers a grant program to subsidize operations, programming, and capital improvement projects at affiliate organizations.

An 11-member commission governs OET and sets it course as a unique planning, operating, and funding agency. The governor appoints commissioners for staggered four-year terms. The agency staff is divided among engineering, programming/traffic, education services, radio reading services, and administration.

Employee Retirement Systems

Retirement benefits, disability payments, and benefits to dependents of deceased employees are paid for all public employees through one of the five state retirement systems, each of which is under the direction of its own board. These are the *Public Employees Retirement System*, the *State Teachers Retirement System of Ohio*, the *School Employees Retirement System*, the *Police and Fireman's Disability and Pension Fund*, and the *State Highway Patrol Retirement System*. Benefits are financed by contributions of members, employers, and income from investments of the funds.

Participation in one of the employee retirement systems takes the place of participation in federally mandated systems such as Social Security. The only exception is that employees hired after April 1986 and their employers must contribute to Medicare.

The *Ohio Retirement Study Commission* looks at the administration and financing of the state retirement systems. It makes recommendations to the General Assembly on an ongoing basis. The commission consists of 14 members appointed by the governor, Ohio House, and Ohio Senate as well as representatives from the public educational institutions, public retirement systems, and state and local government.

State Employment Relations Board

Legislation enacted in July 1983 made Ohio the 40th state to establish a systematic collective bargaining process for public sector employment. Public sector employees, with the exception of safety forces such as police and fire workers, are permitted to strike if the collective bargaining process fails.

The State Employment Relations Board (SERB) was created to administer the provisions of the law. It is responsible for enforcing a uniform standard for every major phase of the collective bargaining process.

The three-member board is appointed by the governor and serves staggered six-year terms. SERB's staff conducts elections to decide union representation issues, determines if probable cause exists in unfair labor practice charges by either union or management, and provides mediation, fact finding, and conciliation services to resolve impasses in collective bargaining issues.

SERB has an informational service in which every public sector bargaining agreement negotiated within the state is analyzed and entered into a computer database for use in further collective bargaining. Ohio is the only public sector bargaining state to provide such a service.

Ohio Ethics Commission

The Ohio Ethics Commission was created as a part of the Ohio Ethics Law of 1973. The six-member bipartisan Ohio Ethics Commission is appointed by the governor to administer and enforce the Ohio Ethics Law and financial disclosure requirements. Its jurisdiction includes all state elected or appointed public officials and public employees, except legislators and judges. The Ohio Ethics Law prohibits public officials and employees from misusing their official position to benefit themselves, their family members, business associates, or others where there is a conflict of interest.

The Ethics Commission administers the financial disclosure statements for most Ohio public officials and employees, including state and local office holders. Financial disclosure statements for judges, judicial candidates, and judicial employees are handled by the Board of Commissioners on Grievances and Discipline of the Ohio Supreme Court, while the Joint Legislative Ethics Committee has jurisdiction over members of and candidates for the General Assembly and employees of the General Assembly.

The commission provides educational sessions and information to the public, issues advisory opinions that interpret the Ohio Ethics law for prospective or hypothetical situations, investigates violations, and holds hearings to refer cases to the appropriate authority for prosecution. All commission investigations are confidential as mandated by law.

Commission on Hispanic/Latino Affairs

The commission was created in 1977 to focus attention on problems of Spanish-speaking people and to advise the governor and General Assembly on developing programs to meet their needs. The commission is made up of 11 members appointed by the governor, some from recommendations by the legislative leadership. All commission members must speak Spanish and be of Spanish-speaking origin.

The Office of Hispanic/Latino Affairs serves as the executive office for the commission. The office also provides information about Spanish-speaking attorneys, translators, and other services to the Spanish-speaking community.

Ohio Historical Society

The Ohio Historical Society, established in 1885, is a nonprofit corporation charged with preserving and interpreting Ohio's history. It maintains a reference library specializing in Ohio history with extensive genealogy collections, along with state and local government records. The society maintains archaeological and historical sites, registries of landmarks, museums, and a research library. In addition, the Ohio Historical Society maintains the state archives of valuable documents and advises local groups on the preservation of their papers and records.

The society is governed by a 21-member board of trustees; nine are appointed by the governor, nine are elected by society members, and three are elected by the board itself. The *Ohio Historic Site Preservation Advisory Board*, appointed by the governor for three-year terms, furthers the preservation of history. The board reviews Ohio's historic preservation plans and recommend sites for inclusion in the National Register of Historic Places.

Inspector General

The Inspector General (IG) investigates allegations of wrongful acts or omissions committed by the executive branch of Ohio government. IG jurisdiction applies to all state agencies and state employees, including state universities and medical colleges. Specifically exempted from IG jurisdiction are the secretary of state, auditor, attorney general, and treasurer, along with their staffs, and community colleges and their employees. These offices have internal divisions that perform the same duties as the Inspector General. The legislative branch falls outside the IG's scope, too, but is under the jurisdiction of the Legislative Inspector General. The Inspector General is appointed by the governor and confirmed by the Ohio Senate.

The IG takes written complaints regarding unlawful acts from all sources, including the public. Complaints are kept confidential during the investigation. They become part of the public record upon completion of the inquiry. If during an investigation the IG finds evidence of wrongdoing, the case is referred to an appropriate law enforcement agency.

Lake Erie Commission

The Lake Erie Commission was established in 1990 to focus additional attention and resources on the preservation and restoration of Lake Erie. Members of the commission include the director of the Ohio Environmental Protection Agency and the directors of the departments of Natural Resources, Agriculture, Health, Transportation, and Development.

The six-member commission is served by a professional staff that prepares for the governor an annual "State of the Lake" report that documents the health of the lake and makes recommendations for improving the lake area. The staff also administers the grant program that provides funds for Lake Erie research and preservation projects. Funds for these grants are raised through private funds and the sale of Lake Erie license plates.

Legal Rights Services

In 1986, the General Assembly created the Ohio Legal Rights Services (OLRS) to protect and advocate for the rights of people with mental disabilities. It serves as Ohio's federally designated protection and advocacy system, as well as its Client Assistance Program. Through these federally mandated programs, and some state-mandated programs, OLRS provides information and referral, counsel and professional advice, and representation on a broad spectrum of cases involving discrimination, abuse, neglect, or rights violations of mentally disabled Ohioans.

In addition to casework, OLRS focuses on advocacy to change laws, policies, or conditions that adversely affect people with disabilities.

State Library of Ohio

The origins of the State Library of Ohio date back to 1817. The State Library of Ohio was originally established to meet the information needs of legislators and state officials. It has extended its services to all Ohioans by assisting in the provision and coordination of library facilities and services throughout the state. The library, located in Columbus, offers a variety of services to other libraries, institutions, and individuals. It provides a special library to meet the work-related needs of state agencies. Additional services include a computerized catalog, a 9,000-volume genealogy collection, inter-library loan processing, library services in state-supported institutions, book-mobiles for rural areas, and special services for people with disabilities.

The State Library of Ohio is a member of OhioLINK, a consortium of 85 university and college libraries throughout the state that offers access to more than 39 million holdings, online patron borrowing services, delivery service of books that are not available on site, and access to online research databases and Internet sources. Additionally, the Ohio Public Library Information Network (OPLIN) is under the purview of the state library board. OPLIN provides Ohioans free Internet access and access to reference databases at each of Ohio's 250 public libraries. OPLIN provides technical support and training for library employees to maintain the network and ensure that all citizens have equal access to information, regardless of the location or format of the information or the location of the user. OPLIN is served by an 11-member board of trustees, appointed by the state library board, each of whom serves three-year terms.

The state library board is made up of five members appointed by the State Board of Education for five-year terms. The library board establishes policies on organization and operation of the library and appoints a state librarian to administer the library. The board is also responsible for a state-wide program of development and coordination of library services.

State Lottery Commission

Voters approved a constitutional amendment in May 1973 to institute a state lottery, and legislation later that year set forth provisions for the Ohio Lottery. The lottery has become a two-billion-dollar-a-year business that generated more than $641 million for primary and secondary education in fiscal year 2003. An executive director of the Ohio Lottery, appointed by the governor, has administrative authority over all lottery operations. A nine-member State Lottery Commission, also appointed by the governor, advises the director and has rule-making responsibilities. Day-to-day operations of the lottery are conducted from commission headquarters in Cleveland. The lottery maintains nine regional offices throughout the state.

Lottery tickets are sold through retail outlets by licensed agents. The Ohio Lottery can spend no more than 20 percent of its revenues in agent commissions, advertising, and administration. The remainder is split between prize winnings and education funds. Ohio law requires that at least 50 percent of each dollar of ticket sales revenue be awarded as prizes and 30 percent be deposited in the state's Lottery Profits for Education Fund. In the 2002 fiscal year, winners received almost 58 percent of every dollar in ticket sales, and 33 percent of every dollar went into the Lottery Profits for Education Fund. Approximately five percent of every dollar went to agents for commissions, and five percent was allocated for advertising and administration.

Office of Criminal Justice Services

The Office of Criminal Justice Services works to enhance the quality, fairness, and efficiency of Ohio's criminal and juvenile justice policy; directs funding to implement support system priorities as established by the governor; and coordinates the implementation of unified justice information systems.

Personnel Board of Review

In 1959 the General Assembly established the Personnel Board of Review, a neutral body to oversee the preservation and protection of civil service law. The board hears administrative appeals affecting state employees, county agencies, and general health districts. The board responds to inquiries from the general public, civil service commissions, and attorneys regarding civil service law and procedures.

The board consists of three members appointed by the governor for overlapping six-year terms.

Power Siting Board

The Power Siting Board, under the administrative umbrella of the Public Utilities Commission of Ohio (PUCO), reviews applications for construction of major power plants and transmission lines in Ohio and issues or denies construction certificates. No major utility facility may be built without obtaining a certificate for the facility. Public hearings are held before the decision to issue each certificate, at which time citizens may give testimony and, in some cases, become parties to the hearing. Voting members of the board are the PUCO chairperson; the Ohio EPA director; directors of the departments of Health, Development, and Natural Resources; and a public member who is an engineer. Four legislators serve on the board as nonvoting members.

Professional Boards

A number of boards have been established by law to determine the qualifications necessary for admission to the practice of a particular profession or skill in Ohio. The boards conduct examinations, issue licenses, and collect fees from eligible candidates. Members are appointed by the governor, and most are required to have professional qualifications in the field. Examples include the Counselor and Social Worker Board, the State Board of Registration for Professional Engineers and Surveyors, and the Board of Examiners of Architects.

Ohio Public Defender Commission

In 1976 the General Assembly created the Ohio Public Defender Commission to provide a comprehensive system of legal representation for indigent persons at state expense. Indigent persons may not be imprisoned for any offense if they have not been represented by counsel. Counsel must be available for interrogations and present for parole revocation hearings unless that right is waived.

The commission is bipartisan and consists of nine members, five appointed by the governor and four by the Ohio Supreme Court. More than half of the commissioners must be lawyers. The commission establishes standards for indigence and appoints a state public defender to coordinate and supervise public defense systems at the local level to ensure that they meet standards set by the commission. A county may establish its own public defender system, or it may make payment directly to counsel selected by the indigent or appointed by the court. Counties are reimbursed for up to 50 percent of the total cost of the operation.

Public Utilities Commission of Ohio

Ohio exercises regulatory power over businesses that deliver services considered essential to the public welfare. The Public Utilities Commission of Ohio (PUCO) regulates the rates and services of electric, natural gas, water, and waste water providers. PUCO also has jurisdiction over telephone, trucking, moving, and railroad services. A utility or transportation company cannot initiate or eliminate a service, modify an existing service, change the rates charged for a service, or expand its service areas without PUCO approval. Municipally owned utilities, cooperatives, or utility companies not operated for profit are not under PUCO jurisdiction.

The commission consists of five commissioners appointed by the governor from a list of qualified candidates submitted by a broad-based nominating council. At least one commissioner must be a lawyer admitted to the bar of any state. No more than three members of PUCO may be of the same political party. Commissioners serve five-year terms and are prohibited from representing a utility before the commission or any state agency for two years after leaving the commission.

Beginning in 1983, PUCO implemented the Percentage-of-Income Plan, which limited low-income clients' bills during the winter months to not more than 15 percent of their total income, allowing them to pay the balance later. Other PUCO programs are the Economic Recovery Program, with special rates for new or expanding industries, and the Self-Help Program, which allows large-scale gas users to buy directly from the pipelines.

> ## PUCO and Cell Phones
>
> *Although the PUCO regulates local telephone service, it does not regulate cellular phone service. Brochures regarding the cell phone utilities and industries are available from PUCO at 1-800-686-PUCO (7826) or online at http://www.puco.ohio.gov.*

In recent years, the PUCO has developed and implemented several programs to bring competition to the local telephone and natural gas industries. In 1999, the Ohio General Assembly and the governor approved a bill that deregulated the electric utilities in the state of Ohio. Although the PUCO will no longer regulate the competitive services supplied by electric utilities, electric transmission and distribution services remain subject to PUCO regulation.

Public Works Commission

The Ohio Public Works Commission (PWC) was created in 1989 to assist in financing local public infrastructure improvements under the state Capital Improvements Program and the local Transportation Improvements Program. The commission must be reauthorized every ten years by the legislature. The commission consists of seven members appointed by the legislative leadership. There are four nonvoting members: the directors of the departments of Development and Transportation and the directors of the Water Development Authority and the Ohio Environmental Protection Agency.

The PWC provides grants, loans, and financing for local debt support and credit enhancement. Eligible projects include improvements to roads, bridges, culverts, water supply systems, waste water systems, storm water collection systems, and solid waste disposal facilities. Projects are recommended to the commission through one of the state's 19 Public Works Districts. The PWC can fund only two to three percent of needed projects, so selection for funding is done on a priority basis. Each district determines its own scoring criteria.

Board of Regents

The state first established higher education institutions with Ohio University at Athens in 1804 and Miami University at Oxford in 1809. By 2004, there were 13 public universities, seven medical schools, and 46 two-year public technical and community colleges and university branches.

Created in 1963, the Board of Regents is the state's planning and coordinating agency for higher education. It is not a governing board, as the individual colleges and universities are governed autonomously by their own boards of trustees, but it does have certain authority over the development of higher education. The nine members of the Board of Regents are appointed by the governor to nine-year terms. Three members are appointed every three years. The chairs of the education committees of the Ohio Senate and House are *ex-officio* members. The board appoints a chancellor who is the chief administrative officer.

The Board of Regents is responsible for formulating a master plan for higher education at five-year intervals. It may approve or disapprove establishment of new branches, state community colleges, area community colleges, and technical colleges. All private colleges or out-of-state institutions wishing to offer courses toward a degree in Ohio must receive authorization from the board to operate in Ohio. The Board of Regents, upon recommendation from each institution, must review and approve or disapprove all new degree programs at public and private institutions.

Each of the 13 public universities is chartered separately and governed by a nine-member board of trustees appointed by the governor. There are seven medical schools in Ohio, five established in conjunction with major universities and two freestanding medical colleges. There are 15 community colleges, eight technical colleges, and 23 university branches. There are 70 private colleges and universities in Ohio that receive some specialized forms of state aid, notably financial aid for students. There are about 285 proprietary (for-profit) schools. The *State Board of Proprietary School Registration* registers proprietary schools after investigation of their facilities and programs.

Financial responsibilities of the board include reviewing appropriation requests from all state-supported institutions and presenting a comprehensive request to the legislature for funds for all higher education. The board recommends allocations of funds for capital development.

The Ohio legislature appropriates higher education subsidies in the biennial operating budget. These subsidies are based on the financial resources available and on a formula including fixed versus variable costs, the kinds of programs being offered, the number and educational level of students enrolled in the programs, and performance-based criteria. Though variable from one institution to another, state subsidies support about 45 percent of the cost of a resident Ohioan's undergraduate education at state-supported colleges and universities; the student pays approximately 55 percent. The level of state support has dropped over the years. Each college or university sets its own tuition. Community and technical college boards of trustees have the authority to place tax levies on the ballot for voter approval. As a result, students may pay lower tuitions at these schools.

Funds for capital improvements for higher education come from "lease-rental" bonds. (See the section on the capital budget in Chapter 8 for a description of these bonds.) These bonds are supported by a pledge of student fees. In actual practice, the debt service is met by a legislative appropriation and is charged directly against the higher education operating budget. Lease-rental bonds make continuing capital improvements programs possible without seeking voter approval of periodic bond issues.

Rehabilitation Services Commission

The Rehabilitation Services Commission (RSC) is a state agency charged with assisting citizens with disabilities in finding employment. RSC is directed by a seven-member commission appointed by the governor. No more than four members may be from the same political party. Three members must be representatives from the rehabilitation profession, including one member from the field of services to Ohioans who are blind. At least four commissioners must be individuals with disabilities, including no fewer than two and no more than three who have received vocational rehabilitation from a state agency or the Veterans Administration. An administrator, appointed by the commission, approves, executes, and recommends agency policies, goals, long-range plans, and future programs.

Two RSC bureaus provide eligible Ohioans with vocational rehabilitation (VR) services to prepare them for employment. The **Bureau of Services for the Visually Impaired** (BSVI) serves people who are blind or have severe visual impairments, and the **Bureau of Vocational Rehabilitation** (BVR) serves people with all other types of disabilities. Counselors in both bureaus work with clients to develop individualized rehabilitation programs that may include continuing education, specialized job training and on-the-job training, work adjustment training, and job placement. Both bureaus also provide tools and equipment to those in need of assistive technology or adaptive devices in order to obtain employment. Anyone can refer a person to one of the more than 60 RSC offices throughout Ohio.

A third division, the **Bureau of Disability Determination** is responsible for determining the eligibility for Ohio's Social Security Disability Determination and Supplemental Security Income claims on behalf of the federal Social Security Administration.

Several advisory groups contribute to the Rehabilitation Services Commission. A 37-member Consumer Advisory Council, which includes persons with disabilities, parents of persons with disabilities, and professionals in the rehabilitation field, provides guidance and input concerning programs offered by the commission.

A 21-member *Governor's Council on Disabled Persons* is housed at the commission and advises the governor's office and the legislature on issues relating to persons with disabilities. It works with public and private employers to facilitate the hiring of individuals with disabilities. Council members are appointed by the governor, and a majority of the members must be people with disabilities.

Rural Development Partnership

The Rural Development Partnership is an advocacy agency of the Ohio Department of Agriculture that brings together citizens, representatives of the private sector, and all levels of government. The partnership is geared toward identifying and communicating the needs of rural Ohioans. Issues that most concern the partnership include agriculture, education and training, economic development and transportation, infrastructure, health, and the environment.

State Racing Commission

The five-member Ohio State Racing Commission appointed by the governor is responsible for the regulation of horse racing in the state. The commission establishes and enforces administrative rules for pari-mutuel wagering at commercial racetracks and fairs; issues permits to thorough-bred, harness, and quarter horse tracks; and licenses all individuals employed or participating in Ohio's horse racing industry. The commission appoints a full-time executive director whose responsibilities are defined in the Ohio Revised Code.

Of the money wagered on horse racing, approximately 79 percent is returned to bettors. The balance goes to permit holders, jockeys, and state taxes. Taxes collected are used to fund commission operations, supplement the PASSPORT Fund (an alternative to nursing home placement), and promote the horse racing industry.

Tuition Trust Authority

In 1989 the General Assembly created the Tuition Trust Authority to over-see the Ohio Prepaid Tuition Program. This program allows Ohioans to purchase tuition units at current tuition prices for use in the future at any of the nation's institutes of higher learning, based on weighted averages. The program is backed by the full faith and credit of the Ohio government.

The authority is led by a nine-member board. The chancellor of the Board of Regents serves on the authority along with four members appointed by the legislative leadership and four members appointed by the governor.

Water Development Authority

The General Assembly created the Water Development Authority in 1968 to provide financing to local governments for projects related to solid waste, water supplies, and water pollution controls. It issues private activity bonds for sewage facilities, solid waste facilities, and hazardous waste disposal facilities. The authority raises revenue for project financing through the sale of municipal revenue bonds, through loans to local governments, and from the issuance of revenue bonds for qualified projects.

The authority is managed by a five-member board appointed by the governor.

CHAPTER EIGHT

Financing State Government

G overnment is financed by citizens. The budget is an economic plan of how money is collected and allocated. There are two major budgets created by the state, the operating budget and the capital budget. Each budget drafted covers two fiscal years (FY). A state fiscal year begins on July 1 and runs through June 30 of the following year. The fiscal year is designated by the calendar year in which it ends; for example, the period July 1, 2004, through June 30, 2005, is FY 2005. All states are required by law to balance their budget.

Operating Budget

The operating budget is the fiscal plan the state government creates to cover the general aspects of state government operations.

In odd-numbered years the governor is responsible for presenting the Executive Budget to the General Assembly. This is the proposed financial plan for the next biennium (two-year period). In practice, the legislature usually divides the Executive Budget into three bills: Operating Budget, Highways Budget (which includes transportation and public safety), and the Bureau of Workers' Compensation Budget (which includes both BWC and the Industrial Commission).

Nationally, there has been an overwhelming trend on the part of states toward using annual budgets. Ohio is the largest state that continues to use biennial budgeting. Budget requests are received from each department and coordinated by the Office of Budget and Management, which prepares the budget request for the governor. A proposed operating budget is introduced in the Ohio House of Representatives because all revenue proposals must originate there. The budget bill goes through the normal legislative process of hearings and debates in the House, then the same in the Senate, a conference committee if necessary, followed by approval of the governor. The General Assembly is responsible for actual appropriations for specific programs and for levying sufficient taxes to ensure that revenues are available to pay for the programs authorized.

After passage of the budget, the Office of Budget and Management is responsible for monitoring and controlling the expenditure of funds. The budget passed by the General Assembly and signed into law by the governor is still nothing more than a plan based on expected revenues and expenditures. If economic conditions shift and revenues do not meet expectations, expenditures must be cut to conform to actual revenues. The governor must invoke such measures as are necessary to bring spending into balance with state income because the Ohio Constitution requires that the budget be balanced at the end of each biennium. In times of economic prosperity, revenues may exceed budgeted expectations, but spending remains as appropriated.

A seven-member *Controlling Board* provides continuing legislative oversight and control of state agency expenditures, operations, and appropriations. Members include three representatives from the House of Representatives and three senators from the Senate. These are the chairs of the finance committees, plus one majority member and one minority member from each house. The director of the Office of Budget and Management, or the director's designee, serves as chair. Ohio law gives the Controlling Board the power to approve transfers of funds within state agencies and from one fiscal year to another. The board may waive competitive bidding require-

The Line Item Veto

Most state governors, including Ohio's, have the ability to use a provision known as the "line item veto." The line item veto provision allows the governor to veto a part of a bill while signing the rest of the bill into law. In 1996 the U.S. Congress passed a law granting the president the power to use the line item veto. However, the U.S. Supreme Court ruled that the line item veto at the federal level was unconstitutional. Ohio's governors continue to use it at their discretion.

ments if it decides an emergency exists, and it may authorize a state agency to transfer capital appropriations for other capital projects. The board controls the emergency-purposes account in the biennial budget and may transfer these funds to meet any agency's unexpected expenditures. Transfers, however, cannot be made for programs not authorized by the General Assembly, nor may the Controlling Board take actions that do not carry out the legislative intent of the General Assembly. The legislature frequently inserts "subject to Controlling Board approval" in legislation, which gives the board additional authority over specific agencies and programs.

Structure of the Operating Budget

The state uses hundreds of separate funds, much like checking accounts, to manage its finances. Each fund has a revenue source or sources, and each fund makes payments for designated state programs, services, or projects.

The largest state fund is the General Revenue Fund (GRF). All revenues coming into the state treasury that are not allocated by law to a specific fund or purpose are deposited into the GRF. The GRF receives 64 percent of total state revenues.

Most of the GRF revenue comes from state taxes levied on sales, corporations, and personal income. In FY 2003, the sales tax provided 28.5 percent of the GRF revenue. This tax is imposed on each retail sale, lease, or rental of tangible personal property in Ohio, unless specifically exempted, and on some selected services. In response to the 2004 budget shortfall, the General Assembly extended the sales tax imposed on services to include dry cleaning, storage, delivery, and personal care services. This extension of the

---

The Tobacco Settlement

In 1998, Ohio and 45 other states signed the Master Settlement Agreement with the nation's largest tobacco manufacturers. As a result, Ohio will receive payments made by the tobacco companies in perpetuity. The amount of the annul fund is subject to several adjustment factors, including inflation and volume. Estimate are that Ohio will receive $298.5 million in payments and interest for FY 2005 and $290.9 million for FY 2006.

Legislation passed in 2000 (SB 192) established Ohio's long-term plan. It created a number of funds for managing tobacco revenue and established the formula for distributing the money among the funds. Trust funds were created for biomedical research and technology, education facilities and technology, law enforcement improvement, community development, tobacco use prevention and cessation, and several public health priorities. The plan requires the governor to recommend in even-numbered years a biennial budget for use of the funds.

The General Assembly diverted tobacco revenue to the General Revenue Fund to balance the 2004-05 operating budget.

tax base reflects Ohio's transition from a manufacturing-based economy to a service-based economy. The corporate franchise tax provided about 5.8 percent of revenue to the GRF in FY 2003. This tax is collected based on the net worth or net income of corporations, whichever is greater. The personal income tax was established in 1972 and accounted for 33 percent of the GRF revenue in FY 2003.

The state received approximately 22.5 percent of its total GRF revenue from the federal government in FY 2003. In FY 2004 this money was for specific programs/services, many of which require state matching funds. Late in federal FY 2003, however, the federal budget provided temporary state fiscal relief for 2002 and 2003. This helped overcome the severe fiscal shortfalls most states were experiencing.

Taxes levied on cigarette sales accounted for 2.7 percent of the GRF. The remaining GRF revenue came from money collected from licenses, fees, permits, the sales of bonds and notes, interest accumulated from investments, and profits from the sale of liquor. Profits from the sale of lottery tickets are also deposited into the GRF; however, voters passed a constitutional amendment in 1990 mandating that at least 30 percent of lottery profits go into the Lottery Profits for Education Fund, another budget fund that finances primary and secondary education.

Taxes may be increased during the budget process by legislative action or by initiative petition for constitutional amendments.

As most state revenues are deposited into the GRF, it is the principal fund through which operating costs of the state government are paid and from which most state services are financed. Approximately 39 percent of the GRF was paid for public assistance and Medicaid in 2003. Another 36.7 percent of the GRF was spent on primary, secondary, and higher education. GRF money is also used to reimburse local governments for local revenue lost through homestead exemptions and rollbacks—two property tax relief programs enacted by the legislature. In FY 2003 this amounted to 5.8 percent of the GRF.

Other major funds in the operating budget include the Highway Operating Fund (four percent) and two internal accounting funds. The overall state budget includes a number of types of restricted funds either generated by specific revenue sources (the Wildlife Fund, Workers' Compensation Fund) or that finance specified activities.

Internal service funds pay for the purchase, at cost, of the services of one government agency from another. Enterprise funds cover the costs of services to the public where such expenses are expected to be reimbursed by user charges (Lottery Fund, Liquor Control Fund). Debt service funds exist to pay interest and principal on state debt incurred from the sale of bonds. Finally, agency and distribution funds account for assets held by the state as trustee or agent for other government units, as in the case of the various retirement funds.

The charts on page 102 show a breakdown of GRF revenue ("sources") and expenditures ("uses"), while the chart on page 101 shows total state expenditures for the 2003-2004 fiscal year.

Capital Budget

Expenditures of $25,000 or more for physical renovation or alterations or for the purchase of land, buildings, or permanent equipment are handled in the state's capital budget.

The Office of Budget and Management drafts a capital budget on the governor's behalf in even-numbered years to finance capital improvements. The process of developing the capital budget is much like that of the operating budget. However, the capital budget differs from the state operating budget in two distinct ways. Capital projects generally have a high initial cost that cannot be funded with current revenues. Furthermore, the capital budget is restricted in how revenue can be raised and how expenditures are made. To meet these two conditions, capital projects are financed with revenues generated through state-issued bonds.

Bonds are interest-bearing loans made to the state. Bonds help to spread the cost of construction across several years, generally seven to 20 years, thereby making construction projects affordable. Bonds are classified by the account that is charged with repayment. Four major classifications exist: general obligation bonds, which are backed by the full faith and credit of the state and therefore can be repaid from any type of state revenue necessary; revenue (special) bonds, which are repaid from revenues, fees, or payments received by the state for the use of the facilities; bonds paid from the General Revenue Fund; and bonds paid from other state funds.

The *Sinking Fund Commission* and the treasurer of state oversee the issuance of the state's general obligation bonds and provide management control over the state general obligation debt. General obligation bonds issued by the Sinking Fund Commission finance highway construction and improvements, parks, recreation and natural resource projects, and coal research and development projects. The state treasurer issues general obligation bonds that finance local government infrastructure improvement projects. Members of the commission are the governor, auditor, secretary of state, treasurer, and attorney general. The timing and size of bond issues are based on authorizations made by the legislature and must comply with constitutional limits on state debt.

A number of authorities have been created by the General Assembly to issue revenue bonds for financing specific types of capital projects. These include the *Ohio Turnpike Commission*, the *Ohio Higher Education Facility Commission*, the *Ohio Housing Finance Agency*, the *Ohio Water Development Authority*, the *Petroleum Underground Storage Tank Release Compensation Board*, and the *Clean Ohio Fund*. The bonds issued are payable from the revenues of the facilities rather than tax monies. They are not included in the governor's budget and are not classified as debt under the constitutional limit.

Bonds paid from the General Revenue Fund are issued and managed by three organizations: the Ohio Public Facilities Commission, the Ohio Building Authority, and the Schools Facilities Commission. These bonds are issued to lenders who receive "lease-rental" payments made from the General Revenue Fund. This means that debt service payments are subject to biennial appropriations made in the state's operating budget under leases or

The Clean Ohio Fund

In 2000, voters approved a bond issue establishing the Clean Ohio Fund. The $400 million program's objective was to clean up polluted areas known as "brownfields" and to preserve green space. In 2001, the fund was activated by the Ohio General Assembly for four years, with provision for periodic renewal up to 25 years. The fund was established by revenue bond, to be repaid by pledged liquor proceeds, or the gross profit on the sale of spirituous liquor. The following components were established with specific purposes and four-year spending authorizations:

- *Clean Ohio Green Space Conservation Program — $150 million for conservation to purchase open spaces and protect green space.*
- *Clean Ohio Trails Fund — $25 million to increase access to outdoor recreation by expanding the number of nature trails.*
- *Clean Ohio Revitalization Fund — $175 million to evaluate and clean up brownfields.*
- *Other — $25 million to preserve farmland; $25 million to address sites contaminated by petroleum and other hazardous substances.*

OHIO GOVERNMENTAL EXPENDITURES

STATE DOLLARS SPENT FISCAL YEAR 2003-2004

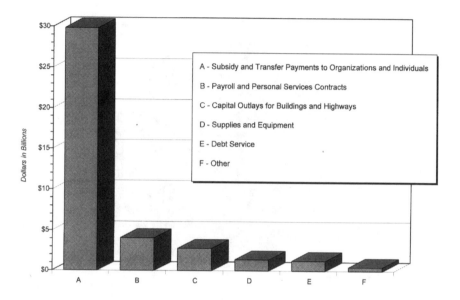

Source: The Ohio Budgetary Financial Report for the Fiscal Year Ended June 30, 2004,
Ohio Office of Budget and Management

---

agreements entered into by the state. The owners or holders of these special-obligation bonds are not given the right to have excises or taxes pledged to the payment of debt service. Bonds of this type are issued to finance capital projects for mental health, higher education, parks and recreation, correctional, and various office facilities.

Bonds paid from other state funds include the Economic Development Bond, which is repaid from profits generated through the state's sale of liquor; the Highway Infrastructure Bank, which is repaid from federal highway payments; and the Ohio Bureau of Workers' Compensation Building, which is financed by revenues of the BWC administrative funds.

GENERAL REVENUE FUND SOURCES
FISCAL YEAR 2003-2004

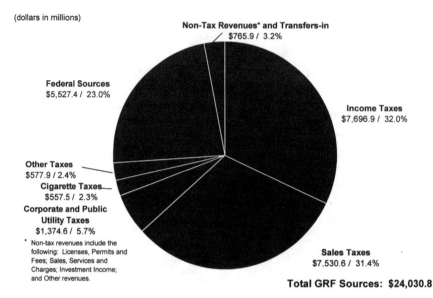

(dollars in millions)

Non-Tax Revenues* and Transfers-in
$765.9 / 3.2%

Federal Sources
$5,527.4 / 23.0%

Income Taxes
$7,696.9 / 32.0%

Other Taxes
$577.9 / 2.4%

Cigarette Taxes
$557.5 / 2.3%

Corporate and Public
Utility Taxes
$1,374.6 / 5.7%

* Non-tax revenues include the
following: Licenses, Permits and
Fees; Sales, Services and
Charges; Investment Income;
and Other revenues.

Sales Taxes
$7.530.6 / 31.4%

Total GRF Sources: $24,030.8

GENERAL REVENUE FUND USES
FISCAL YEAR 2003-2004

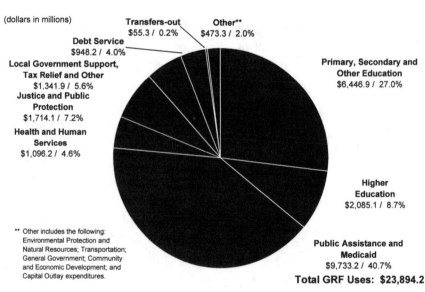

(dollars in millions)

Transfers-out
$55.3 / 0.2%

Other**
$473.3 / 2.0%

Debt Service
$948.2 / 4.0%

Local Government Support,
Tax Relief and Other
$1,341.9 / 5.6%

Justice and Public
Protection
$1,714.1 / 7.2%

Health and Human
Services
$1,096.2 / 4.6%

Primary, Secondary and
Other Education
$6,446.9 / 27.0%

Higher
Education
$2,085.1 / 8.7%

** Other includes the following:
Environmental Protection and
Natural Resources; Transportation;
General Government; Community
and Economic Development; and
Capital Outlay expenditures.

Public Assistance and
Medicaid
$9,733.2 / 40.7%

Total GRF Uses: $23,894.2

Source: The Ohio Budgetary Financial Report for the Fiscal Year Ended June 30, 2004,
Ohio Office of Budget and Management

CHAPTER NINE

Local Government

All political power originates with the people. When the United States of America was founded, the people delegated certain powers to the new federal government. The U.S. Constitution defines what powers were delegated. Those powers not specifically delegated to the federal government were reserved by the states. The states grant specific powers to local governments through state constitutions and statutes. However, some forms of local government existed in Ohio before the first state constitution was adopted in 1802.

Two features make Ohio's system of local government distinctive. One is the very strong home rule provisions for municipalities. The other is the constitutional limitation of ten mills on unvoted property tax. This ten-mill limitation is known as "inside millage." Additional tax millage, or "outside millage," must be approved by voters to provide necessary funds for local government operations.

Ohio now has more than 3,600 separate local government units and ranks sixth among the states in the total number of units. The Ohio Constitution authorizes three major types of local government units: municipality, county, and township. A fourth type in use in Ohio is the special district. Special districts are authorized by state law and are created by decisions of local officials or by a vote of the people. For example, school and health districts are classified as units of local government.

Understanding Home Rule

Article 18 of the Ohio Constitution grants certain powers to municipalities. The General Assembly cannot interfere with powers granted to municipal corporations by the Ohio Constitution unless the Constitution sanctions their interference. On the other hand, municipal laws cannot be in conflict with laws passed by the General Assembly. Municipal "home rule" powers include the power of local self-government, the exercise of certain police powers, and the ownership and operation of public utilities beyond its borders.

Municipalities

Ten city governments were organized under the Northwest Ordinance of 1787. After passage of the first constitution, cities were chartered individually with special laws passed for each one. This procedure wasted legislative time and gave different treatment to the various municipalities. The 1851 constitution prohibited special legislation and required the General Assembly to pass general laws governing organization of all cities and villages. After passage of these laws, cities pressed for legislation that would enable them to meet the special needs of their people. This resulted in a population classification system with 11 different classifications of cities. The Ohio Supreme Court declared this system unconstitutional in 1902. The General Assembly responded with adoption of a new municipal code with only two classifications of municipalities. But pressure by large cities for more flexibility continued, and in 1912 the people approved the present Article XVIII of the constitution, which allows municipal corporations to have home rule power.

Form

The form and powers of municipalities in Ohio are specified in the constitution and the Ohio Revised Code. In general, Ohio municipalities provide the services usually associated with local government: police and fire protection, water supply, traffic control, public health regulation, and sanitation. Municipal corporations are classified as cities if their population exceeds 5,000; otherwise, an incorporated municipality is called a village. There is no other classification according to population. The secretary of state declares the status of a municipality as a city or a village following the federal decennial census.

Three alternative methods are provided by which municipalities may be organized: (1) according to provisions of the general laws, (2) according to the optional plan laws, or (3) by a home rule charter.

The general laws provide for the mayor-council form of government. In this form the mayor is the chief executive officer, and a council, varying in size with the size of the municipality, is the legislative body. Several other executive officers are elected, and the mayor appoints the heads of the other executive departments. There is a difference between the prescribed form for an incorporated village and for a city, although both might be considered "weak mayor" forms of government with executive authority divided between the mayor and either a commission or other elected officials.

The optional plan laws provide for specific variations of each of the three basic forms of government. These are the mayor-council form; the council-manager form, in which an elected council determines general policy and appoints a manager to administer it; and the commission form, in which executive and legislative functions are combined in one elected body. An optional plan must be approved by the electors. This option has never been used extensively in Ohio, probably because home rule charters were made possible at the same time.

"Any municipality can frame and adopt or amend a charter for its government and . . . exercise thereunder all powers of local self-government," according to Article XVIII, Section 7, of the Ohio Constitution. It is under this home rule authority that cities and villages may adopt charters that vary their form of government from those offered under the general and optional plan laws. A proposal to frame a charter may be submitted to the electors by either a two-thirds vote of the legislative authority of the municipality or must be submitted upon petition of ten percent of the electors. Charter issues can be voted on at either a general or special election at which voters decide whether they want a charter to be drawn. In the same election electors vote for the 15 charter commissioners who will write the charter if the issue passes. The commission must submit the proposed charter to the voters at a time of its own choosing within a year of its election. The charter becomes effective if it is approved by a majority of the electors voting. Home rule charters may vary as to council size, method of election, number of executive officers and departments, etc., to meet the needs and wishes of the community. About two-thirds of Ohio's cities operate under home rule charters.

Powers

In addition to providing flexibility in the form of government, the 1912 amendment gave home rule powers to municipalities. Home rule means simply the authority to govern your own affairs. The home rule amendment granted this power to all municipalities regardless of size. Both charter and noncharter municipalities have home rule power, although court decisions have tended to grant more power to charter municipalities than to noncharter municipalities.

Section 3 of Article XVIII states: "Municipalities shall have authority to exercise all powers of local self-government and to adopt and enforce within their limits such local police, sanitary, and other similar regulations as are not in conflict with general laws." Since 1912 the meaning of this section has been tested hundreds of times in the courts to determine which are municipal powers and which are state powers. Generally, municipalities have full power over the internal operation of their municipal government—the departments, boards, commissions, and so on. In addition, they have the authority to regulate the behavior of their citizens provided these regulations are not in conflict with state laws. State law takes precedence over municipal ordinance in any area that could be considered to affect the health and welfare of all citizens; for example, municipalities have little ordinance power over the regulation of fireworks.

Other sections of the constitution state that the General Assembly may pass laws limiting the powers of municipalities to levy taxes or incur debt and that municipal electors have initiative and referendum power over municipal ordinances. Municipal corporations may appropriate property for public use and may sell any excess so acquired; assess property that benefits from local improvements to pay for such improvements; and own and operate a public utility, sell up to 50 percent of the product of the utility outside its own corporation limits (water and sewer services are not subject to the limitation), and issue mortgage bonds to acquire or extend the utility.

Municipalities may provide police and fire protection; municipal electric power, heat, and water supply; libraries, hospitals, and places of correction; and public landings, wharves, docks, and piers. They may establish and care for streets, regulate vehicles and the use of streets, impound animals, regulate sanitation, provide for refuse disposal, and regulate weights and measures. Municipalities may construct the necessary buildings for police and fire use, purchase fire engines or boats, build airports, provide off-street parking, rehabilitate blighted areas, and build limited access highways or freeways. The power to care for streets includes the right to assess benefited property owners. Municipalities may plan for the development and use of all land within the city limits and may implement this plan through zoning regulations. All these specific powers are included under the general grant of power by the constitution.

Incorporating and Dissolving

New villages can be formed by petition to the county commissioners of a majority of land owners in the area to be incorporated. Hearings must be held. County commissioners, however, cannot allow the incorporation if the territory involved is within three miles of an existing municipal corporation unless that municipality approves or has rejected annexing the territory. The area of the proposed village must be at least two square miles, have a population of 800 persons per square mile, and have an assessed property valuation of $3,500 per person. A special provision is included in state law that permits a township area with a population of 25,000 or greater to incorporate as a city even though the proposed incorporation would include territory within three miles of an existing municipality. The question of incorporating as a city must be approved by the electors.

A village automatically becomes a city upon reaching a population of 5,000 according to the federal decennial census and by declaration of the secretary of state. A village may be dissolved as a corporation on petition of 40 percent of its electors and an affirmative vote at an election called to consider the question.

The County

The Northwest Ordinance of 1787 provided the basis for organization of ten counties in Ohio. The number of counties increased rapidly after adoption of the first constitution in 1802 until the last of the present counties was organized in 1851.

Ohio's 88 counties vary in size from 228 (Lake County) to 702 (Ashtabula County) square miles, and in population from 13,128 (Vinton County) to 1.38 million (Cuyahoga County). The county was created to serve as an agency for the administration of state law. Some of the state functions counties administer are justice, human services, elections, maintenance of land records, and tax collection. The major difference between counties and municipalities is that a municipality is created by the state upon request of the people living within it for their interest, convenience, and advantage, but counties are created by the state, without the consent of the people, in order to carry out state policy. A municipality is a stronger form of government in Ohio since all municipalities are granted home rule power by the constitution.

Form and Powers

County government structure is clearly outlined by state law unless county electors have adopted a home rule charter or approved a form of government under the alternative forms law. All counties in the state are organized under the general law, except Summit County, which adopted a charter form of government in 1979.

For counties in Ohio, the General Assembly has prescribed a commission form of government headed by a three-member board of county commissioners elected to overlapping four-year terms. The commissioners have responsibility for both policy making and policy execution in the county. Except for Summit County, there is no elected county executive head, although commissioners may appoint an administrator. Commissioners share the executive function of the county with eight other independent county officers: auditor, clerk of courts, coroner, engineer, county prosecutor, recorder, sheriff, and treasurer. These officials, who are also elected by the people to four-year terms, are technically the equals of the commissioners, whose major control over them is through the county budget.

The commissioners are responsible for the county's financial management as well as facilities maintenance, personnel administration, and economic development. They approve the annual budget and determine tax levies for county purposes and bond issues for county capital improvement. They may also grant tax abatements. They may buy and sell land and buildings, manage real and personal property, and provide necessary county buildings. They approve annexations and municipal incorporation and in some counties are responsible for rural zoning. They have a wide range of human service responsibilities, including the administration of federal and state workforce investment programs. County departments

Why 88 Counties?

When Ohio was established, the early state leaders wanted to ensure that the government was accessible to the citizenry. Therefore, the 88 counties were created, each with a county seat that could be reached within one day's journey on horseback.

under their control usually include building regulation and inspection, purchasing, sanitation engineering, human services, budget, and dog warden. Commissioners have major responsibilities to assure that solid waste is properly managed and have responsibility for storm water drainage and ditch improvements.

Although counties originally existed strictly as state administrative agencies, they are now developing quasi-municipal functions. Their legal existence and powers are dependent on the state. The scope of county powers was increased when the state granted commissioners the authority to enter into agreements with a municipality, a special district, a township, or another taxing authority to perform any service provided by that body. The flexibility possible under this power provides one means of solving some of the problems facing metropolitan areas today.

Duties of the county officers are specified by law. The **auditor** determines the tax value of property, maintains county financial records, and issues warrants for payment of county obligations. The **treasurer** collects taxes in the county and its subdivisions, disburses expenditures, invests the county's funds, and collects delinquent taxes. The **recorder** records deeds, mortgages, plats, liens, and other written instruments.

The **county prosecutor** is the chief legal officer of the county, investigating and prosecuting crimes committed within the county. The prosecutor also acts as attorney in defending the county in court and giving legal advice to county agencies and townships. The coroner determines the cause of death of persons dying in a violent or suspicious manner and issues death certificates. The **sheriff** is the chief law enforcement officer and custodian of the county jail while also providing services to the courts.

The **engineer** is responsible for the construction, maintenance, and repair of all bridges in the county, and for county roads and other public improvements except buildings. The **clerk of courts** is responsible to the appellate and common pleas courts, entering judgments and collecting court costs. The clerk also issues and transfers automobile and water craft certificates of title.

Other Forms of County Government

A constitutional amendment adopted in 1933 and modified in 1978 gives the people of a county the right to adopt a home rule charter. The charter outlines the form of government, the officers to be elected, and the procedure for performing state-mandated duties. It may provide for organization of the county as a municipal corporation and for municipal powers to be exercised by the county.

A charter commission elected by the people frames the charter and submits it for a vote, or citizens may, by initiative petition, submit a charter to the electors. The charter needs only a majority vote unless it provides for the exclusive use by the county of a municipal power. In that case it must be approved by majorities of the voters in all of the following: a) in the county, b) in the largest municipality, c) in the county outside the largest municipality, and d) in a majority of the combined total of municipalities and townships of the county. The fourth majority is not required in counties with a population of 500,000 or greater.

By popular vote in November 1979, Summit County became the first of Ohio's 88 counties to adopt a home rule charter. The charter, placed on the ballot by citizen initiative, replaced the three-member board of commissioners with an elected county executive and county council. The new charter government took effect in January 1981.

The constitution also gives the state legislature authority to provide by general law alternative forms of county government for adoption by the people.

A law was passed in 1961, and considerably strengthened in 1967, to permit counties to have an elected or appointed county chief executive and to vary the size and method of election of the commission. Finance, personnel, and law departments may be created, and the government may exercise all powers implied by state law provided there is no conflict with municipalities. However, none of the other eight elected county officers can be eliminated. The people must approve a proposal for an alternative form by a majority vote.

County Boards and Commissions

The number of boards and commissions in any county varies according to the needs of that particular county. The **County Budget Commission**, composed of the auditor, treasurer, and county prosecutor, has the responsibility for reviewing the tax budgets of all subdivisions in the county to be sure they comply with the Ohio Constitution and statutes. The section entitled "Financing Local Government" in this chapter describes the operation of this commission in more detail.

The auditor, treasurer, and president of the board of county commissioners make up the **Board of Revision**, which hears and investigates complaints relating to the valuation or assessment of real property. The board may revise assessments. Appeals from its decisions may be filed in common pleas court or with the *State Board of Tax Appeals.*

Other county boards include education; elections; health; children's services; airport authority; mental retardation and developmental disabilities; planning; zoning; and alcohol, drug addiction, and mental health.

Townships

Townships were first laid out in Ohio according to the basic policy for the survey and sale of public lands established by Congress in the Articles of Confederation in 1785. This system of townships, six miles square subdivided into sections one mile square, has been used in surveying most public land ever since. After the first Ohio Constitution was adopted, the legislature tended to follow the original survey lines in creating townships. The present 1,309 townships in Ohio are divisions within the counties. All land areas not incorporated into municipalities lie within the jurisdiction of a township.

The constitution provides for township government, but it is up to the General Assembly to prescribe its form and powers. Townships are managed by a three-member elected board of trustees and a township clerk. Townships can only exercise those powers specifically delegated to them by the General Assembly. A township may engage in economic development; grant tax abatements; buy and sell land; and adopt noise, animal, right-of-way, and weed-control regulations.

Townships are required to provide basic services to their residents. The care and maintenance of the township road system is the largest function of townships today. Townships are responsible for 44,000 miles of roadway in Ohio, more than the counties, municipalities, and state. Other services provided include fire and police protection, emergency medical services, parks and recreation, zoning, and cemetery management. Township trustees also have responsibilities for ditches, drains, culverts, and line fences between adjacent properties.

All townships begin as "basic" townships. Basic township responsibilities include road maintenance, police and fire protection, and cemetery management. Recently, the General Assembly created "limited home rule" townships. When a township has reached a population of 5,000, the citizens can elect to adopt a limited form of self government, including funding a sheriff and prosecuting attorney. This limited home rule provision allows township government expanded local legislative authority and more power to enforce township resolutions. Townships with a population between 5,000 and 14,999 must submit the question of limited home rule to electors of the township for approval. Townships with a population exceeding 15,000 may submit the question to the electors of the township or the trustees can adopt limited home rule by a unanimous vote. A trustee vote to adopt limited home rule may be contested and put before the voters if a petition is submitted to the township trustees. This petition must include signatures equal to ten percent of the number of citizens in the township who voted for governor in the last gubernatorial election. Those townships that adopted limited home rule by unanimous vote of the trustees and have a population exceeding 15,000 are designated as "urban townships." Urban townships have the authority to adopt access management regulations in addition to other limited home rule authorities.

Financing Local Government

The state constitution and state law define the system of taxation used to finance the approximately 3,600 local governmental units in Ohio.

Administration

The county auditor, under supervision of the state Department of Taxation, is responsible for valuations of real property in each county. Real property in Ohio is taxed at 35 percent of its true market value. Reappraisals of property valuations are made every six years and updated every three years. The valuations of public utilities and businesses are certified to the county by the state tax commissioner.

Local budgets and tax rates are established by the taxing authority of each local government. This authority prepares an estimate of income and expenditures for the following year and sets a tentative tax rate. Public hearings are held, and the budget must be adopted by July 15 and filed with the auditor by July 20. These budgets are reviewed by the County Budget Commission to ascertain if tax levies are properly authorized. Tax rates are adjusted as necessary, and a final legal tax rate for each local government is set. After the tax rates are determined, the list is sent to the treasurer, who bills taxpayers twice a year. Tax funds are also distributed to the local governmental units twice a year.

What's a Mill?

A mill is a unit of measurement used in calculating the tax rate for some taxes based on property or net worth. A mill is one tenth of a penny. A mill produces $1 in tax revenue for every $1,000 of the taxable value of the property or net worth against which it is levied.

The County Budget Commission allocates portions of the Local Government Fund to counties, municipalities, and townships, by statutory calculations. Appeals from commission decisions may be filed with the State Board of Tax Appeals and from there to the Ohio Supreme Court.

Sources of Funds

Local governments are limited by law as to how they collect and disburse funds. Counties and municipalities have been granted the authority to impose a broad range of taxes by the General Assembly. Townships have limited taxing authority.

Certain revenue funds must be spent on particular services. These are known as "earmarked," restricted, or special-purpose funds. Other funds that are collected can be spent at the discretion of the local government. These funds are known as discretionary funds, or general purpose funds.

Taxes constitute the largest revenue source for local governments. Additionally, governments generate revenue from fees and licenses, fines, and court costs. Local government units may also be eligible for various state and federal monies for specific programs. Some taxes are levied directly by the local government, while others are state-imposed taxes that are returned to the local level by the state government. The Local Government Fund is a special fund that transfers a percentage of revenues from state sales, income, and corporate franchise taxes to local governments. This money is distributed to municipalities, counties, and townships according to statutory formulas.

County

The real property tax is the largest single source of local revenue. It is paid on real estate, on public utility property, and on tangible personal property used in business. The Ohio Constitution allows local government to impose a personal property tax of up to ten mills, known as "inside millage." Local governing bodies can also place a tax levy on the ballot for consideration by the citizens residing in that governmental unit. This is known as "outside millage." Revenue from property taxes is deposited into general purpose funds or special purpose funds, based on how the tax was assessed. If the revenue was generated based on inside millage, the money goes to the general purpose fund. However, if the revenue was generated based on outside millage, the money goes to the special purpose fund for which the levy was passed.

Counties generate further general purpose funds by levying a county sales tax. The county sales tax is in addition to the sales tax levied by the state. County sales tax rates range from an additional .025 percent to 2.0 percent. Both the state and county sales taxes are collected at the same time, and the state returns the county portion to the county from which it was collected.

Other major sources of tax revenue include motor vehicle license tax, real estate transfer tax, tangible personal property tax levied on businesses, public utilities property tax, lodging tax, and the manufactured home tax.

Municipalities

Taxes are a major source of revenue for municipalities. Not all tax revenue is collected by the municipality itself. The county and state collect various taxes on behalf of the municipality and share the revenues according to statutory requirements.

The county assesses and collects personal property taxes from county residents and businesses. The county treasurer returns a portion of the tax revenues to the municipalities within the county.

Portions of certain taxes levied by the state are returned to municipalities. The Local Government Fund disburses 5.8 percent of the total state-levied sales, income, corporate franchise and public utility excise taxes to municipalities. Thirty-four percent of the state-levied motor vehicle license fee is returned to municipalities, while state gasoline taxes are returned based on the number of registered drivers residing in the municipality. Sixty-four percent of the Ohio estate tax is refunded to the municipality in which the tax originates. Municipalities benefit from several other taxes, including the house trailer tax and the grain handling tax. These taxes represent only a small portion of the total revenue. The state shares in the revenue generated from certain licenses and permits. Liquor permits and pawnbroker licenses are two of the major sources in this category.

Municipalities raise further revenue through local taxes and fees. Municipalities are permitted to impose an

> ## Property Values and Taxes
>
> *Example: A school district that levies a 23 mill property tax in an area that has an average property valuation of $100,000 will raise twice as much revenue as a school district that levies a 23 mill property tax in an area that has an average property valuation of $50,000.*

income tax on all income earned within their boundaries and by their residents. A one percent tax may be levied by resolution of council. Higher rates require the approval of voters. A hotel/motel tax of three percent can be enacted to fund a convention and visitors' bureau or a sports facility.

Municipalities can assess fees for court costs, parking meters, inspection services, building permits, public utilities, and licenses. These fees are levied primarily to cover administrative costs.

Townships

Townships have limited authority to generate income. However, townships can assess fees for township contracts, permits, and services. The majority of township revenue comes from inside millage and other property taxes levied by the township for services provided. State funds, including those in the form of the local government funds, make up another significant portion. Townships receive funds from the motor vehicle fuel tax, motor vehicle license tax, and the estate tax.

Expenditure of Funds

Each form of local government disburses its revenues according to what services it is authorized to provide. County and municipal governments provide a wide variety of services, whereas townships provide a limited number of services.

Counties are responsible for providing police protection, emergency services, judicial services, road maintenance, solid waste management, health and human services, economic development and planning, as well as information services. Municipalities provide many of these same services and therefore must fund their operation.

Townships, with a more limited array of services, generally fund police, fire, and rescue services; road and bridge maintenance; zoning; and capital improvements and maintenance.

School District Organization

Education is a state responsibility. In Ohio, much of the control over schools has been delegated by the General Assembly to independent government units called school districts. These districts must comply with state laws and regulations; however, they have broad authority over how funds are raised and spent.

Each area of the state is located in one of three kinds of school districts: city, local, or exempted village. City school districts enjoy the broadest authority, while local districts have the most limited authority. City school district boundaries do not always coincide with municipal boundaries. Educational service centers serve local school districts in the county by providing services that are not economically feasible within the individual school districts. City and exempted village districts do not participate in this pooling of resources.

Two or more districts may combine to provide a vocational school for all persons within the area. Such a district is called a joint vocational school district or JVS.

Each school district has an elected board of education—except for Cleveland, where the mayor appoints the school board and selects the superintendent. In all other cases, an elected board of education is responsible for hiring the superintendent, teachers, and other necessary personnel; providing equipment; and directing the many aspects of school administration. The board may place tax levies and bond issues on the ballot and impose a local income tax for schools, as necessary, to provide for an adequate operating budget in the district and for construction of needed buildings. Board members are elected on a nonpartisan ballot for overlapping, four-year terms. The JVS board consists of representatives from the boards of participating school districts.

In 2002-03 there were 197 city, 373 local, and 49 exempted village districts. There were also 49 joint vocational school districts and 60 Educational Service Centers. Because of overlap between joint vocational districts and traditional school districts, the State Department of Education officially recognized 615 school districts in Ohio. Beyond these public school districts, by May 2004 the department recognized 183 community, or charter, schools serving more than 48,000 students.

The *DeRolph* Decision and School Funding in Ohio

In March 2003, the Ohio Supreme Court ended the judicial debate over school funding in Ohio by granting a writ of prohibition. A writ of prohibition is a judicial writ from a higher court ordering a lower court not to exercise jurisdiction in a particular case. In this case, the Supreme Court ordered a writ of prohibition against the Perry County Court of Common Pleas exercising jurisdiction over the DeRolph *case.*

The case law generated in DeRolph *I and II clearly states that the responsibility for securing a "thorough and efficient" system of common schools falls upon the state, and that "thorough and efficient" is a high standard of quality for all schools. Out of this lawsuit, a number of changes have been made to school funding in Ohio:*

- *A $23 billion program to rebuild and renovate schools through the Ohio School Facilities Commission has been established.*

- *Parity aid was added to the school funding formula to address disparities among rich and poor districts. In Ohio, school funding relies heavily on the use of property taxes, which leads to some disparities. For example, school districts with larger tax bases and higher property values generate more funds for schools than districts with smaller tax bases and lower property values.*

- *The percentage of the state's general revenue budget allotted to public K-12 education has increased from 34.5 percent in FY 1992 to 39.3 percent in FY 2003, a $1.2 billion increase.*

- *A Blue Ribbon Task Force on Financing Student Success was appointed by the governor to develop a constitutional system for funding schools. The task force was scheduled to release its report and recommendations in the fall of 2004.*

Financing the Schools

Funding for education is addressed in Article VI of the Ohio Constitution, which states that "the General Assembly shall make such provisions, by taxation or otherwise, as, with the income arising from the school trust fund, will secure a thorough and efficient system of common schools throughout the state." The system of funding education in Ohio is a shared responsibility between state and local governments. The state provides funding through the Education Budget Bill, while local school districts generate income from local taxes.

There are federal grants available for specific programs, including special education, vocational education, gifted education, and education for disadvantaged pupils. Additionally, school districts can qualify for federal funds for at-risk students, Head Start, and school lunch programs.

The No Child Left Behind Act (NCLB), signed into law in 2002, made substantial changes in the role of the federal government in establishing guidelines for public school funding and performance. The General Assembly passed legislation in 2003 to bring Ohio into compliance with NCLB, but questions remain regarding lack of adequate funding from the federal government and lack of flexibility in the performance standards.

State Funding

Since 1920, the state has contributed money to local school districts under various formulas. Many changes have taken place as successive legislatures have tried to determine the best and fairest ways to distribute state tax money and to determine the extent to which the state should try to equalize differences among districts. The challenge is to provide quality education for all public school children.

State funds are allocated by the legislature according to a distribution formula aimed at equalizing the per pupil expenditure in school districts throughout the state. The state share is adjusted based on local contributions. The legislature establishes the total amount of state and local revenue per-pupil that the state considers a school district needs in a given fiscal year to provide an adequate education to its students. In FY 03, this amount was $5,058 per pupil. This amount is multiplied by a cost-of-doing-business ratio and an average daily membership ratio. For example, if local revenue were generated based on a hypothetical 23 mill tax rate, the adjusted total taxable property value would be subtracted to produce the amount that the state would contribute per pupil to school districts. Each district receives a different amount, based on the contributing factors used in the formula calculation.

Local Funding

Most of the local money for education comes from taxes levied on property. The amount a school district can raise varies widely among districts, depending on property tax rates and property values within the district. Levies to raise additional outside millage to fund schools must be approved by voters. Voter attitudes play a large role in funding schools in Ohio. In 1989, school districts were authorized to get voter approval to levy a local income tax as an additional source of funding for schools. By 2003, 126 out of 615 school districts had approved the income tax option for schools.

Health Districts

Health districts are local government organizations that provide direct health services mandated by the Ohio Department of Health. The state is divided into health districts according to the type of local government and population. Each city is designated a city health district; villages and unincorporated areas within a county are combined into general health districts. Cities may elect to combine with a general health district in order to provide health services more economically and efficiently.

As of 2003, there were 88 county and 49 city health departments making up Ohio's 137 local health departments. There were 184 city health districts that were either combined or contracting with these 137 local health departments. With a few exceptions permitted by city charters, each health department is governed by a board of health. The boards of health must implement the services mandated by the Ohio Department of Health, as well as meet the unique needs of the population in their respective health districts. The board of health is responsible for hiring a health commissioner, who is responsible for directing the services of the department.

Most boards are comprised of five members appointed for five-year terms. Combined health departments are permitted to set terms and numbers of board members according to their contracts. General members of a board of health in a combined district are appointed by a district advisory council made up of the president of the county board of commissioners or county executive, village mayors or chief executives, and chairpersons of boards of township trustees in the county. City board of health members on either city or combined district boards are appointed by the city chief executive with approval of the city council.

Funding

Federal funds constitute a major part of local health department funding. These funds include grants to local health departments for special programs and block grants that are channeled through the Ohio Department of Health. Major federal block grants currently channeled to local departments include the Maternal and Child Block Grant and the Preventive Medicine Block Grant.

Local funds raised through property taxes and fees are earmarked for use in providing local health services. In general health districts, the board of health submits its budget to the county budget commission for approval, and funding comes from township and village revenue.

The state provides a small subsidy and other funds for specific health programs, provided the local health department meets the optimal standards established by the Public Health Council to assure local services are being provided. This subsidy is approximately $0.32 per resident and has been at this level for the past two decades.

If all other funding sources prove inadequate to fund necessary general public health programs, the county board of health may request up to a one mill levy.

Special Districts

State law has authorized the creation of a variety of special districts to serve specific governmental purposes. A special district has an independent budget and means of financing. It is established in response to a need for a specific service not offered already within the boundaries of an existing governmental unit. Each type of special district is authorized by a separate law; districts are usually single-purpose.

The chart on pages 120-123 shows the types of districts authorized by Ohio law, their method of establishment and financing, and the appointment of their governing bodies.

SPECIAL DISTRICTS

Type and Purpose	Creation	Governing Body	Financing
Conservancy Districts (flood control, water supply, sewage disposal)	Petition of landowners or governing bodies to Common Pleas Court	Appointed by common court	Issues bonds; assessments
Joint Township Hospital Districts	Boards of trustees of participating townships	All members of boards of trustees of participating townships	County & township appropriations; charges with voter approval
County Library Districts	County Commissioners and referendum	Appointed by county common Pleas & county commissioners	State general funds; property tax levies
Regional Library Districts	Joint resolutions of commissioners of two or more counties	Appointed by the county commissioners in participating counties	Library and Local Government Support Fund; property taxes
Area Library Service Organizations	Resolution of board of trustees of two or more counties	Appointed by county commissioners in participating counties	Federal, state, and local funds; contracts
Metropolitan Library Service Districts	Agreement among board of trustees of four or more libraries in a metropolitan area & approval of State Library Board	Members of governing bodies of participating libraries	Federal, state and local funds; contracts

Major River Watershed Districts	Participating counties file map/description with Ohio EPA & Secretary of State	Appointed by county commissioners; board of directors representing the public, agriculture, industry, public water supply and public recreation	Prorated among counties on value of real & personal property
Metropolitan Housing Authorities (public housing)	State director of development	Appointed according to formula by common pleas & probate court, county commissioners, chief executive officer & legislative authority of certain municipalities within the district	Issues bonds; service fees; grants & contributions
Joint Ambulance Districts	Resolution of governing bodies of participating townships and municipalities	Selected by governing bodies of participating governments	Charges; levy property taxes & issue bonds with voter approval
Joint Fire Districts	Resolution of governing bodies of Participating townships and municipalities	Selected by governing bodies of participating governments	Property tax levies with voter approval
Joint Fire & Ambulance Districts	Joint resolution of joint ambulance district & joint fire districts that share the same service area	Selected by governing bodies of participating governments	Service fees; levy property taxes & issue bonds with voter approval

SPECIAL DISTRICTS (CONTINUED)

Park Districts	Petition of electors or public governing bodies to Probate Judge	Appointed by Probate Judge	Issue bonds; assessments; levy property taxes with voter approval
Township Park Districts	Common pleas court on the petition of electors to township trustees & referendum	Appointed by common pleas court or by board of trustees	Levy property taxes & issue bonds with voter approval
Port Authorities	Ordinance, or resolution of municipality, township, county or combination	Appointed as determined by agreement of participating government bodies	Service charges, levy property taxes & issue revenue bonds with voter approval
Regional Airport Authorities	Resolution of county commissioners of one or more counties	Appointed by county commissioners	Issue revenue bonds, rental and service charges
Regional Arts and Cultural Districts (operates cultural facilities; support art and cultural organizations)	Resolution of county or combination of counties, cities or townships by board of county commissioners	Appointed by governing bodies of participants or in populous counties by board of county commissioners	Grants; issue general obligation bonds; service fees; levy property taxes and issues bonds with voter approval
Regional Transit Authorities (provide transit facilities for ground, air, and water transportation)	Resolution of governing bodies of two or more municipalities, townships, or counties	Specification for selection set by resolution creating; members appointed by appropriate governing body	Grants; issue general obligation bonds; service fees; levy property tax & sales tax with voter approval

District	Created by	Governed by	Powers
Regional Water and Sewer Districts (provide sewage disposal; water supply)	Petition of one or more municipalities or counties or common pleas court	Selected in manner determined by each district	Service fees; assessments; issue bonds; levy property taxes with voter approval
Regional Solid Waste Management Authorities	Resolution of one or more counties after approval from municipalities and townships within counties	Appointed by governing bodies of participants	Service fees; issue revenue bonds
Sanitary Districts (provide sewage & garbage disposal; water supply)	Petition of one or more municipalities or counties to common pleas court	Appointed by common pleas court	Issues bonds; service charges; assessments
Soil and Water Conservation Districts	Mandatory in each county	Elected board of supervisors	Donations; gifts; assessments; state aid, county general fund contributions; tax levies with voter approval
Transportation Improvement Districts	Resolution of boards of county commissioners	Appointed according to specifics of resolution	Federal & state aid, assessments; service fees; issue revenue bonds with voter approval
Joint Solid Waste Management Districts	Resolutions of board of commissioners of participating counties	Boards of commissioners of participating counties (or if no commissioners, three people appointed by the legislative body)	Service fees; issue revenue bonds

CHAPTER TEN

Elections and Political Parties

O f all the responsibilities of a representative democracy, the right to vote is fundamental. This process enables people to select the officials who will make, administer, and interpret the law. Article V of the Ohio Constitution is entitled Elective Franchise; it sets forth who may vote, specifies the type of ballot to be used in general elections, and establishes the direct primary. The statutes regulating voting and elections have been adopted by the General Assembly and can be found in Title XXXV of the Ohio Revised Code. They are administered primarily by the secretary of state, who is the chief elections officer.

In 2002 the federal government enacted the Help America Vote Act (HAVA). This wide-ranging election-reform legislation to improve the operation of elections requires statewide computerized voting lists, "second-chance voting," provisional ballots, and access for people with disabilities. HAVA moves much of the responsibility for the elections from the local level to the states.

Voting

Who May Vote

A person who is a citizen of the United States, 18 years of age on or before the day of the election, a resident of the state for 30 days before the election, and registered at least 30 days before the election is qualified to vote in Ohio. For voting purposes, the law defines residence as the place "in which one's habitation is fixed and to which whenever one is absent, one has the intention of returning." Citizens who will be 18 by the November election date are eligible to register to vote and participate in the primary elections, even though they may be 17 at the time of the primary election; however, 17-year-olds may not vote on issues.

Persons convicted of felonies lose their voting eligibility while incarcerated. When discharged or granted probation, parole, or pardon, their voting rights are restored. A person may be determined to be incompetent to vote by a probate judge following a judicial procedure.

Registration

Registration with the state is required by the Ohio Constitution in order for citizens to vote. There are more than 7.1 million registered voters in Ohio. Registration lists are maintained by county boards of elections, but under HAVA they must now conform to a statewide database. There are a variety of places where citizens meeting the above requirements can register in person to vote: their county board of elections or designated branch offices established by the board of elections; the Office of the Secretary of State or other designated state agency offices; any branch of the Bureau of Motor Vehicles; any public library, public high school, or vocational school; or any county treasurer's office. Additionally, citizens can register to vote by mail through the secretary of state's office or their local board of elections. Mail-in forms may be distributed anywhere, by anyone, at any time.

Registration made in person or by mail must be received or postmarked 30 days prior to an election to be valid for that election. If the 30-day deadline is missed, the registration is still processed, but the citizen does not have the right to vote in the upcoming election. Voter registration is maintained unless the elector changes address, changes names, or fails to vote in a four-year period.

Those who move or change names and wish to remain registered to vote must report such changes to their local board of elections via one of the options listed above for registration. Voter registration can be updated through the courts when a name change occurs due to marriage or a court order by

Voter Registration and Identification

Persons registering to vote by mail after January 1, 2004, must provide identification information when attempting to vote for the first time unless *the person provides his/her current Ohio driver's license number or the last four digits of his/her Social Security number on the registration form. The identification information is either a copy of a current and valid photo identification showing the voter's name or a copy of a current utility bill, bank statement, paycheck, government check, or other government document showing name and address. However, if the voter registration is taken (not mailed) to the board of elections, identification and proof of residency are not necessary.*

filing a "change of voting status." These types of changes must be filed with the state 30 days prior to an election. However, citizens who have moved within their county may report the change and vote at the board of elections during the absentee voting period, or may appear at their new polling location. Those who have moved from one county to another within the state may report the change and vote at their county board of elections in the county to which they have moved.

Electronic Voting in Ohio

In response to HAVA requirements, the state of Ohio began making the transition from punch card ballots and lever voting machines to electronic voting machines or optical scan ballots. A variety of electronic voting machines exist; most require voters to touch a portion of a screen to cast their vote. Optical scan ballots are voted by filling in an oval or completing a broken arrow by a candidate's name. All voting systems still have provisions for write-in candidates. By 2006, all Ohio counties are to ensure that their new voting system maintains a voter-verifiable paper trail of ballots cast.

Absentee Voting

Ohio statutes permit anyone to vote an absentee ballot who is 62 years of age or older, expects to be absent from the county on Election Day, is unable to go to the polls because of physical disability or illness, will be unable to vote because of observance of a religious belief, is confined in jail awaiting trial or serving sentence for a misdemeanor, is hospitalized or attending a family member who is hospitalized, is on active duty with the state militia, or is a poll worker or election official. There are special provisions for an armed services absentee ballot. Those who wish to vote by absentee ballot must give their name and voting address, reason for voting absentee, mailing address, and signature.

Citizens who meet the above circumstances may request an absentee ballot by mail from their board of elections, or voters may choose to appear in person at the board of elections during the absentee voting period. Absentee ballots may be requested after January 1 until the day before the election. Ballots are not mailed until 25 days prior to the primary election in a presidential election year or 35 days for all other elections. Voters casting an absentee ballot by mail must return it so that the board receives the ballot by 7:30 p.m. on Election Day. As an exception, absentee ballots mailed from outside the country will be counted if postmarked by Election Day and received within ten days after the election. (Absentee voters who want to vote in person rather than by mail can appear at their county board of elections office or designated locations starting 35 days prior to the election.)

Persons who are hospitalized are permitted to vote by medical emergency absentee ballot and may have the ballot delivered and returned by a family member or by two board of elections employees of different political parties. Applications must be received by 3 p.m. on Election Day, and ballots returned to the board by 730 p.m.

Certain electors who have moved from Ohio within 30 days before the election may vote absentee for President and Vice President in the county of their former residence provided they cannot vote at their new residence.

Armed Services Voting

Persons serving in the U.S. armed services, their spouses, and their dependents who move to be with or near the person serving in the military may vote by armed services voter's ballot. They do not have to register to vote, but they must meet all other requirements for voting in Ohio. The place where the person resided when entering the service is deemed the voting residence unless the service member establishes a permanent residence elsewhere. Members of the armed services, spouses, or a close relative may apply for ballots anytime after January 1 of the year of the election by writing, faxing, or appearing before their board of elections. Ballots must be received by the time the polls close on Election Day. If the ballot is mailed from outside the country and postmarked by Election Day, it will be counted if received up to ten days after the election. Service members may also vote in person at the board of elections within 35 days before the election. Military members stationed in this country but outside Ohio may choose to register and vote where they live instead of voting by an armed services ballot.

Overseas Voting

People living overseas should contact the American embassy, consulate, or military installation in the country where they are residing regarding registering to vote overseas and voting absentee.

Provisional Voting

Voters whose names do not appear on the voter registration roll when they arrive at their polling place may vote a provisional ballot, which will not be counted until the voter's eligibility is verified after the election.

If a registered voter has moved form one precinct to another within the same county, the voter can vote in the new precinct on Election Day. Such voters will complete a change of address form and vote.

Registered voters who have moved within their precinct can go to their precinct polling place on Election Day, file a change of address, and vote a regular ballot, which will be counted that night.

If a voter has been registered anywhere in Ohio and moves to a different county within Ohio, the voter should go to the new county board of elections to vote. The voter will complete a change of address and be given a provisional ballot.

Provisional ballots are counted in the official count, starting 11 days after the election. Provisional voters may find out if their ballot was counted by calling a toll-free number, 1-866-644-6868.

Ballots

The Ohio Constitution requires that ballots for general elections have the names of all candidates for an office arranged in a group under the title of the office they seek. This is called an office-type ballot. Names are rotated on the ballot so that, so far as possible, each name appears an equal number of times at the beginning, the end, and in intermediate positions. The party name or designation is printed under or after each name. A voter must indicate—for example, by marking an X, punching a card, pulling a lever, touching a computer screen, or filling in an oval—the name of each individual for whom he or she is voting. In Ohio, it is not possible to vote a "straight party ticket" by marking only one X for all the candidates of one party. In the general election, names of candidates for judge, boards of education, and most municipal or township offices appear on a nonpartisan ballot.

An issue may be brought before the voters at a primary, general, or special election; it may be marked "for" or "against."

Wording of Issues

Ballot wording for statewide ballot issues, including constitutional amendments, citizen-initiated laws, and referenda, is written by the *Ohio Ballot Board*. Created by constitutional amendment in 1974, the five-member board is composed of the secretary of state and four members appointed by the legislative leadership. No more than two of these appointees can be from the same political party. The ballot language prepared by the board may not be found invalid by the courts unless it misleads or defrauds the voters. The Ballot Board is also responsible for writing explanations for those amendments proposed by the legislature and for directing the means by which the secretary of state disseminates information concerning state ballot issues to the voters. The legislature requests proponent and opponent committees to write explanations and draft pro and con arguments for amendments proposed by the legislature or citizen initiative and for laws proposed by initiative. Where a law is contested by citizens who petition to submit it to a referendum, the persons named in the petition write the explanation and arguments against the law. The explanation and arguments in favor of the law in question are written by a committee named by either the General Assembly or the governor. Ballot language, explanations, and pro and con arguments for each statewide issue are published for three weeks prior to the election in a newspaper of general circulation in each county in the state.

Voting Procedure

Citizens are assigned a voting location, based on their voter registration address, by their county board of elections. Voting locations are open from 6:30 a.m. to 7:30 p.m. on the day of an election. Electors enter the polling place, give their name and address to an election judge, and sign the poll list. The signature on the poll list is compared with that in the registration book, and the fact that the elector appeared to vote is noted on the record. Voters who cannot sign their names in the registration book may make a mark to represent their name. Their identity is verified by precinct officials and witnessed by a judge of the polling place. Physically or mentally disabled or illiterate voters may receive help from two poll workers of different political parties or from a person of their choice, although not from an employer or union official. No voter may occupy a booth for more than five minutes when all are in use and people are waiting to vote.

The voting system instructions are posted for operating the voting system in use, and poll workers demonstrate its operation. A *Board of Voting Machine Examiners*, three members appointed by the secretary of state, is responsible for approving all voting equipment before it can be purchased by a county for use in Ohio elections.

Polling places are to be free of barriers to people with disabilities. Voting accessibility in *every* polling place is to be assured, and the facility must comply with the Americans with Disabilities Act.

HAVA provides for "second-chance" voting; that is, the voting system notifies the voter of a possible error, allows the voter to verify his or her vote, and provides an opportunity to correct any error (including issuance of a replacement ballot).

No campaign literature may be displayed or given out within 100 feet of any polling place. However, this does not prohibit a voter from taking a list of the voter's chosen candidates and issues into the polling place.

At any primary, special, or general election, electors may be challenged on grounds of age, citizenship, residence, or a charge of having already voted. The judges of elections, designated "challengers," or any elector lawfully in the polling place may make challenges. Political parties or any group of five or more candidates may appoint a qualified elector to serve as "challenger." These challengers must notify the board of elections 11 days before the election of their appointment.

Elections

The general election for federal, state, and county officers is held on the first Tuesday after the first Monday in November in even-numbered years. Elections for local offices are held on the same day in odd-numbered years.

Presidential-year primary elections (2004, 2008) are held on the first Tuesday after the first Monday in March. Other primary elections are held on the first Tuesday after the first Monday in May in even-numbered years (2006, 2010); in odd-numbered years they are held on the date specified by the charter of the municipality holding the election.

Special elections may be held on the first Tuesday after the first Monday in February, May, or August, or on the day authorized by a particular municipal or county charter for the holding of an election.

Election Officials

Local administration of Ohio election law is based on the theory of bipartisanship, that is, that two competing political parties will cooperate to serve the electors of the state. The secretary of state, as the chief election officer of the state, appoints a *Board of Elections* in each county to administer the law. However, the secretary of state has the power to cast the deciding vote in case the board is evenly divided on an election matter.

Each county board is composed of four members, two from each major political party, who serve four-year terms. The secretary of state appoints one new board member from the two major parties in each even-numbered year. The appointments are chosen from recommendations made by the executive committee of the county central committee of the major parties. After new appointments are made, the board elects a new chairperson from among its members. The board then names a director who must be of the opposite political party from the chair, and may name a deputy director whose party must be opposite from that of the director. Both the board of elections and the costs of holding elections are financed by the county itself.

Among its duties, the board of elections registers voters, maintains records of registered voters, establishes wards and precincts, selects polling places in each precinct, provides election equipment and supplies, reviews and certifies the sufficiency and validity of petitions and candidate nomination papers, prints and delivers ballots, and issues certificates of election (or nomination in primaries) to successful candidates. Each board of elections certifies election results to the secretary of state.

The board of elections appoints election officials who serve one-year terms and staff each of the voting locations within the county. No more than one-half of the officials—or judges, as they are also called—can be from the same political party. These judges are responsible for the direct administration of an election, keeping a record of the voters, giving out and receiving ballots, and counting the votes and reporting them to the board of elections. Officials are provided training by the board of elections using materials provided by the secretary of state.

County boards of elections are responsible for conducting recounts when requested by losing candidates or persons on the losing side of an issue campaign. Applications must be filed within five days after election results are certified and must indicate which county precincts should be recounted. A $10 fee for each precinct to be counted is charged for filing the application. When the winning margin is less than one-half of one percent of the total vote for a local or district office, or one-quarter of one percent for statewide office, a recount is automatically ordered and is publicly funded.

The Primary Election

The primary election is an election to narrow the field of candidates for the general election. In Ohio, the primary is also used to select political party officials and to nominate candidates who will run for office in the general election.

Ohio has a direct, closed primary, which means that candidate voting is limited to those citizens who declare their party affiliation. Nonaffiliated voters may choose to become officially affiliated with a particular party by requesting that party's ballot at a primary election. Voters who have participated in primary elections and wish to change their party affiliation must sign a statement to that effect. However, party affiliation is in no way binding in the general election, where voters may choose whichever candidate they consider most qualified.

Issues may also be voted on at a primary election. Issues are on a separate nonpartisan ballot, and voters may vote on issues at a primary election without stating a party affiliation.

Primaries to nominate municipal officials and judges for the municipal court are held in municipalities as required by municipal charter or state law. A city charter may provide for either a partisan or nonpartisan primary. In nonpartisan primaries, the ballot lists all candidates without party labels, and all voters are eligible to vote for candidates. The two candidates receiving the most votes for each office run against each other in the general election regardless of their party affiliation. In charter municipalities, dates for municipal primary elections are set in the charter.

Party candidates for U.S. President and Vice President are not chosen directly through state primary elections. Instead, these candidates are chosen through a proxy voting system at national nominating conventions held during the summer of presidential election years. State primary election ballots list the name of the party candidates running for office. The state primary election results determine at which nominating convention delegates will be selected.

The General Election

In even-numbered years candidates for the following offices are nominated and elected:

FEDERAL: U.S. President/Vice President to four-year term (2004, 2008); two U.S. senators to six-year terms (2004 and 2006 in Ohio and every six years thereafter); all members of the U.S. House to two-year terms (even-numbered years).

STATE: Governor/lieutenant governor, attorney general, secretary of state, auditor of state, treasurer of state to four-year terms (2006, 2010); half of the state senators every two years to four-year terms; all state representatives to two-year terms; justices of the Supreme Court to overlapping six-year terms; courts of appeals judges to overlapping six-year terms; State Board of Education to overlapping six-year terms. (Most judicial candidates run on partisan tickets in the primary, but the general election is nonpartisan.)

COUNTY: Three commissioners (except in Summit County), auditor, county prosecutor, sheriff, recorder, treasurer, engineer, coroner, and clerk of courts to four-year terms. One commissioner and the auditor are elected in state election years, all others in presidential election years. Judges of the common pleas court and county court are elected to overlapping six-year terms.

In odd-numbered years, municipal and township officials, municipal court judges, and members of local boards of education are elected, the latter on nonpartisan tickets. Constitutional amendments and state and local issues may be placed on the ballot during any scheduled election in any year.

Candidates

Each citizen who chooses to run for elected office must meet a set of prerequisites. All elected positions have a residency and "registered voter" requirement, and most have other conditions the candidate must meet.

Candidates also must file a statement of candidacy and circulate petitions to gather signatures of voters supporting their candidacy. The number of signatures candidates must gather depends on the office sought and on whether they represent a political party or are independent candidates. Party candidates are those who are members of a particular party, whereas independent candidates do not represent any political party. No one may be a party candidate who has voted as a member of a different political party in the last two calendar years, unless it is to become a candidate for a newly formed political party. Party candidates may collect the signatures only of those citizens affiliated with the same political party.

Only registered voters who are residents of the district or political subdivision in which the candidate is seeking office may sign that candidate's petition. They must sign in ink or indelible pencil, and each signature must be followed by the date and place of residence of the signer. Petition circulators must declare that they witnessed the signing of all signatures and that, to the best of their knowledge, they are valid. The petitions are submitted along with a specified filing fee to either the secretary of state's office or the board of elections, depending on the office. Petitions and fees must usually be received 75 days prior to the primary election, in the case of party candidates, or one day prior, in the case of independent candidates.

The secretary of state, or the appropriate board of elections, determines whether a petition has the required number of signatures, and local boards of elections determine the validity of the signatures from their counties. A candidate may withdraw from an election by filing a written statement any time prior to the election. The candidacy of an office-seeker can be protested through the board of elections where the petition was filed. Election officials must schedule a hearing and notify the candidate and those protesting the candidacy. At the time of the hearing, the board determines the validity of the petitions and declares whether the candidacy is valid or invalid.

Judicial Candidates

Ohio judges are elected on a nonpartisan ballot at the general election, but their nomination at the primary election may be either partisan or nonpartisan. Judges of the Supreme Court, courts of appeals, and courts of common pleas are nominated either in party primaries or by petition as independent candidates. Municipal judges are nominated according to municipal charter provisions if the jurisdiction of the court is the same as the municipal boundary. Otherwise, the nomination procedure is the same as for common pleas judges. County court judges are nominated by petition only.

Write-in Candidates

Provision must be made on the ballot for write-in votes for every office, both at the primary and the general election. No votes are counted for the write-in candidate unless that candidate has filed a declaration of intent to be a write-in candidate at least 50 days before the election, met all requirements for the office, and paid the appropriate filing fee for the office sought. The declaration is filed with the secretary of state for a statewide office or with the county board of elections for a district or local office. Write-in candidates for U.S. President and Vice President must also file a slate of presidential electors.

Financing Campaigns

Political campaigns in Ohio are financed generally through contributions from citizens, businesses, political parties, and organizations that support the election of the particular candidate. State campaign finance laws regulate contributions as well as the kind of expenditures that can be paid for with campaign contributions. Ohio law requires candidates, political parties, and political action committees to publicly disclose all contributions and expenditures made each year through regular reports. Recent campaign finance law reforms have established limits on contributions to state political candidates. These contribution limits are revised in January in odd-numbered years.

When an individual becomes a candidate for elected office, the candidate must form a committee immediately and appoint a treasurer. The candidate may decide to be the sole member of the committee; in that case, the candidate is the treasurer of the committee as well. The committee is responsible for receiving all campaign contributions, paying all expenditures, and filing all contribution and expenditure reports. A pre-election report must be submitted by the 12th day before the election if the campaign committee received or spent more than $1,000. A post-election report, due the 38th day after the election, is required of all candidates. An annual report must also be filed if no post-general election report is filed. Reports are filed with either the secretary of state or the local board of elections, depending on the office. Local candidates may be exempt from filing reports, depending on whether they fall below a specified minimum of contributions and expenditures.

Political action committees (PACs), two or more persons who receive contributions or make expenditures to influence the result of an election, including elections on issues, must file pre-election reports 12 days prior to an election if they receive or spend more than $1,000 to influence an election. Lesser amounts need not be reported until the post-election report, which is due 38 days after the election. An annual report reflecting activity since the last required report must be submitted by the last day of January. Where PAC reports are filed is based on the PAC's activities. Those PACs that focus a majority of attention on statewide issues and candidates file with the secretary of state, while locally focused PACs file with the board of elections of the most populous county in the district where they have concentrated their activities.

Political parties must submit pre-election reports 12 days prior to the election if contributions and expenditures exceed $1,000. Post-election reports are due 38 days after an election, and annual reports are due the last day of January as well.

The General Assembly in 1974 created the Ohio Elections Commission (OEC). The seven-member commission oversees political party spending, campaign finance, and corporate political contributions. OEC investigates cases of unlawful campaign practices, including campaign misrepresentation, campaign law violations, and dissemination of political communications with no identification of those responsible for the material. OEC may impose a fine or send the findings of its investigations to the appropriate county prosecuting attorney for action. OEC is also responsible for making recommendations to the General Assembly regarding campaign practices and political spending.

The governor appoints six members to OEC, based on recommendations of the two major party caucuses of the General Assembly. These six members (three from each party) select the seventh member, who serves as chair.

Political Parties

The political party is the organization through which the individual citizens work with others of similar ideas to influence the policies and conduct of government. The functions of the party are to choose candidates to run for office in the general election, work for the nomination and election of its candidates, formulate the party platform or position on issues, carry out party policies, and educate citizens in civic and political matters. When voters declare a party preference at a primary election in Ohio, they are considered members of that political party.

The Ohio Revised Code (ORC) defines a political party as "any group of voters which, at the most recent regular state election, polled for its candidate for governor in the state or nominees for presidential electors at least five percent of the entire vote cast for such office." A political party may be formed when a group of voters files a petition with the secretary of state declaring their intention to organize a political party and participate in the next primary election. The petition must be signed by a number of registered voters equal to one percent of the total vote for governor at the last general election. A new political party may not assume a name that will cause it to be confused with an existing party. No party that in any way advocates the overthrow by force or violence of the local, state, or national government may be recognized or given a place on the ballot. Parties are no longer officially recognized by the state if the party fails to poll five percent of the total vote cast for governor.

The ORC defines three types of political parties in Ohio. A major political party is one whose nominee for governor received at least 20 percent of the vote in the last election. An intermediate party is one whose candidate received between ten and 20 percent of the vote. A minor party is one whose candidate received at least five percent but less than ten percent of the vote or whose candidate has filed a petition signed by one percent of the voters at the last election for governor.

Party Organization

In Ohio, state law outlines the basic organizational structure of political parties and establishes procedures for party leaders.

STATE: Major and intermediate political parties are required to have a state central committee made up of one man and one woman from each congressional district in the state, elected at the primary in even-numbered years. The state central committee is responsible for coordinating party affairs throughout the state, arranging for the state convention at which the party platform is formulated, raising and distributing campaign funds, and determining which candidates shall have party support. Within major parties, the state central committee elects an executive committee and a state chair.

Minor parties have no requirements as to organization but must file an organization plan with the secretary of state if they wish to elect controlling committees at the primary.

COUNTY: Major political parties are required to elect a county central committee in each county, made up of one elected person from each election precinct in the county, or from each ward in each city and from each township in the county, as the outgoing committee determines. The county central committee is responsible for directing party activity within the county, presenting a slate of candidates, and working with the precinct committee to strengthen the party by enlisting active party workers at the precinct level. Precinct committee members are generally elected to four-year terms.

CHAPTER ELEVEN

Citizen Participation in Politics

olitics is the art and science of government. Citizens take part in politics when they voice their opinions on schools or taxes, contribute
money to a candidate or to a cause, join a group backing an issue,
sign a petition, vote, or write their legislators. Citizens may choose to participate in varying degrees and ways. Participation, in whatever form, helps
strengthen the system of self-government.

Voting is the initial and easiest form of participation for most citizens.
Qualifications and procedures for voting are outlined in the preceding
chapter. Further opportunities for political involvement include lobbying and
testifying before the legislature; writing to public officials; participating in
initiative and referendum petition drives; campaigning for issues or candidates; running for office; serving on government boards, commissions, and
committees; monitoring governmental meetings; and litigation. Many
federal programs now require citizen participation in planning how funds
are to be spent.

Contacting Officials

Government officials need to hear from their constituents to better
understand what voters are thinking. There are many ways that citizens can
contact their government officials, including by letter, e-mail, telephone, and
in-person meetings. No matter which method of communication is used, the
guidelines on page 139 should be observed.

Testifying at Hearings

Public hearings are held by state legislative committees on all proposed
laws before they are debated and voted on by the entire chamber. They are
held by state agencies before adoption of rules for administering state laws
as well. Public hearings give citizens, groups, and organizations a chance to
present their views on a proposed law or rule, to give the reasons why they

The Do's and Don'ts

of Contacting Government Officials

Do

- get in contact!
- let government officials know when you agree with them, not just when you disagree.
- be brief and to the point; discuss only one issue, and include a bill reference if possible.
- clearly express your opinions or ideas.
- use your own words to express your opinion.
- include your address and signature.
- be courteous and reasonable.
- make contact early in the session before a bill has been introduced if you have ideas about an issue you would like to see incorporated in legislation. If you are lobbying for or against a bill, and your representative is a member of the committee to which it has been referred, write when the committee begins hearings. If your representative is not a member of the committee handling the bill, write just before the bill comes to the floor for debate and vote.
- contact the chair and members of a committee holding hearings on legislation in which you are interested. While you have more influence with the representative from your own district, you are not precluded from contacting representatives from other districts.
- contact each government official individually; it's courteous and more effective.

Don't

- apologize for contacting them. (Your opinion is not an imposition, and your representative is elected in part to hear your views.)
- begin on the righteous note of "as a citizen and taxpayer."
- be vague.
- be rude or threatening.
- sign and send a form or photo copied letter or e-mail.

think it should or should not be adopted, and to answer questions directly about its effect on them. Individuals do not have to be experts to testify at hearings. An informal statement by a single citizen can be dramatic and effective; those who represent a number of citizens carry still more weight.

Those wishing to testify should notify the chair of the committee just before a hearing begins by filling out a witness slip and returning it to the committee's legislative aide. When called to testify, citizens should begin by stating their name (and the name of their organization if applicable, along with its size and goals) and the basis of their concern with the issue. Testimony should be stated clearly in terms of support or opposition, giving reasons and specific examples from experience. The most effective speakers are calm and direct, taking a positive approach if possible; they are brief and specific and use their own words. Formal statements on behalf of an organization should be in writing, with copies provided to the committee members and to the media.

Hearings are a useful part of the democratic process at every level of government. These guidelines for giving effective testimony before a state legislative committee apply as well to a hearing before a municipal zoning commission, a county budget commission, or any other board or agency.

CORRECT SALUTATIONS AND CLOSINGS

Federal	State
President The President The White House Washington, D.C. 20500 Dear Mr. President: Very respectfully yours,	**Governor** The Honorable [Name] 77 South High Street, 30th Floor Columbus, Ohio 43215-6117 Dear Governor [Name]: Sincerely yours,
Vice President The Vice President The White House Washington, D.C. 20500 Dear Mr. Vice President: Sincerely yours,	**Senator** The Honorable [Name] Ohio Senate Columbus, Ohio 43266-0604 Dear Senator [Name]: Sincerely yours,
Senator The Honorable [Name] United States Senate Washington, D.C. 20510 Dear Senator [Name]: Sincerely yours,	**Representative** The Honorable [Name] Ohio House of Representatives 77 South High Street Columbus, Ohio 43215-6111 Dear Representative [Name]: Sincerely yours,
Representative The Honorable [Name] The House of Representatives Washington, D.C. 20515 Dear Representative [Name]: Sincerely yours,	*For information about contacting other elected officials, see Chapter 12.*

Legislative Lobbying

The laws of the state are passed by the legislature. Lobbying is the art of persuading elected representatives to pass, defeat, or amend laws. Lobbyists perform an essential function in the democratic process. They provide legislators with facts relating to proposed laws and background information that might not otherwise be available. The lobbyist's job is to demonstrate to the legislature that substantial support for/opposition to change exists with the voters.

A person does not have to be paid to be a lobbyist. While many corporations, unions, and associations pay their lobbyists, other groups use volunteers, who are just as effective. There is always opportunity for people who feel strongly about a legislative objective to work for its passage. Good lobbyists should have a thorough understanding of the issue, a commitment to the cause, enthusiasm, sincerity, and a sense of humor. They build rapport and understanding with legislators by personal contact, presenting them with relevant factual material and demonstrating support from constituents.

Ohio law requires all paid lobbyists, or paid persons engaged in influencing legislation during at least a part of their time, to register with the Joint Legislative Ethics Committee (JLEC). Volunteer lobbyists and those lobbying on their own behalf need not register.

DO'S AND DON'TS FOR LOBBYISTS

Do

- recognize legislators as human beings and respect and listen to their views.
- get to know their staffs and treat them courteously.
- identify yourself immediately with each contact.
- know the issue and status of the legislation.
- know the legislators (their past records on legislation, party, position in the legislature, legislative and outside interests).
- commend them for actions you approve.
- be brief, then follow up periodically.
- give legislators easy-to-read materials with important facts highlighted.

DON'T

- be arrogant, condescending, or threatening.
- overwhelm them with too much written material they do not have time to read.
- get into prolonged arguments.

Initiative and Referendum

The Ohio Constitution reserves the right for Ohioans to propose legislation or amendments to the state constitution, called "initiative," and to vote whether to reject laws passed by the legislature, called "referendum." Initiative and referendum provisions are a final protection for citizens who feel the legislature has ignored an important issue or has passed a bad law. These powers are exercised by filing petitions containing the required number of signatures with the appropriate authority.

Constitutional amendments may be initiated directly by the people, bypassing the legislature. A summary of the proposed amendment must be certified by the attorney general. The full text of the amendment and the summary are then filed with the secretary of state. The citizens who initiated the amendment must circulate petitions to collect enough signatures to equal ten percent of the electors voting for governor in the last gubernatorial election. Signatures must come from at least half of Ohio's 88 counties and represent five percent of the total vote cast for governor in that county in the last gubernatorial election. Signatures must be received by the secretary of state no later than 90 days prior to the general election so that the secretary of state, with the assistance of the local boards of elections, can verify the validity of the signatures. The ballot wording, prepared by the Ohio Ballot Board, along with arguments for the amendment prepared by the initiating committee and arguments against it by persons named by the legislature, is published once a week for three weeks in a newspaper of general circulation in each county. If a majority of the voters approve the amendment, it becomes part of the constitution.

Laws are initiated indirectly by the people since the petition must be submitted to the legislature first. Signatures of three percent of the electors voting in the last gubernatorial election are required to introduce the proposed law in the legislature. If the legislature does not pass the law in four months, or if an amended version is passed, the petitioners have 90 days to collect signatures of an additional three percent of the electors and place it on the ballot. Signatures must be obtained from half of the 88 counties. The law is voted on at the next general election 90 days after this second petition is filed and becomes effective if approved by the voters. It is not subject to the governor's veto.

A referendum on a law already passed by the legislature may be requested by petition within 90 days after the law has been filed with the secretary of state. It may not be requested on an emergency law, tax levy, or appropriations for current expenses. Signatures of six percent of the electors voting in the last gubernatorial election are required on the petition and must be obtained in at least 44 of the 88 counties. The law is submitted to the voters at the next general election 60 days after the petition is filed and cannot become effective unless approved by a majority of the voters.

Monitoring the Administration

After laws are passed, the responsibility for administering and enforcing them lies with the executive branch of government. Citizens have a right to know what executive branch officials are doing.

The Ohio Open Meetings Act, referred to as the Sunshine Law, requires public bodies to conduct official business in meetings open to the public at all times. Any prearranged meeting of a majority of members of a governmental body to discuss or conduct public business is a public meeting. Public bodies must establish a method for citizens to learn the time and place of regular or special meetings they hold and must notify the media immediately if an emergency meeting is called. There are several public organizations that are exempt from all Open Meetings Act provisions due to the nature of the organization. They are grand juries, audit conferences, and the Ohio Organized Crime Investigation Commission. Furthermore, certain meetings of the Adult Parole Authority, the State Medical Board, the Board of Nursing, and the Emergency Response Commission are exempt from Open Meetings Act requirements. Several state agencies are also permitted to hold "executive sessions" to discuss confidential information.

Under certain circumstances, other public bodies that are subject to the Open Meetings Act may hold "executive sessions" that are closed to the public. These exempted circumstances include personnel matters, the purchase or sale of public property, collective bargaining issues, security arrangements, and discussions with an attorney regarding pending court actions. Discussion during the executive session does not have to be made public; however, specific motions and their disposition must always be made in open session.

Any person or organization may bring suit in common pleas court against a public body holding or planning to hold an unauthorized closed meeting.

Full and accurate minutes of public meetings must be recorded and open to public inspection. In fact, all public records must be open at all reasonable times for inspection. Any document that records the organization, functions, policies, decisions, procedures, operations, or other activities of a public body is a public record under the law. Persons responsible for public records are required to make copies of them available at cost to anyone requesting them within a reasonable period of time.

Going to Court

Citizens' rights are not automatically self-fulfilling, even though they would seem to be guaranteed by laws or by the constitution. Litigation is a way to determine exactly what those rights and duties are and to ensure compliance with them. Citizen groups increasingly are suing in court to protect public interests.

By forming a coalition with other organizations or by working with a law firm that will handle public interest cases *pro bono*—that is, without charge or at a reduced rate—the expense of initiating a lawsuit can be reduced. Some national organizations take cases they consider to be of public concern without charge, or they have access to low-cost legal aid, such as law school faculties and government-paid legal aid lawyers. If a plaintiff wins the suit, the court may order that plaintiff's attorney's fees be paid by the defendant. Court costs are an additional expense.

A more limited involvement in litigation is that of *amicus curiae* (friend of the court) in a suit brought by another organization or individual. Citizens can submit a legal memorandum on some point on which they have expertise, but have no control over the suit or relief requested. Permission of the court, and often of both parties to the suit, must be obtained.

Appointment to Boards, Commissions, and Councils

Many advisory or policy-making boards and committees include citizens appointed by the governor or an appointing body. A citizen can apply for appointment to one of these boards and, through it, influence state or local decision-making.

Most appointments require knowledge specific to the organization to be appointed. One can, for instance, establish a professional reputation in the field, or actively participate in political life, as in lobbying for a new agency. One can gain knowledge through participation in a reputable volunteer organization such as Common Cause, the Farm Bureau, the American Civil Liberties Union, or the League of Women Voters. These organizations are often asked to nominate a candidate for an ad-hoc or standing committee on a particular problem.

There are various positions that do not require professional expertise. Sometimes a relevant life experience is of prime importance, as in an advocacy council for people with disabilities. Citizens with experience and interest can write to their congressional delegates or other elected officials, give their qualifications, and ask for an appointment.

Advisory boards exist at the local, state, and federal levels.

In Conclusion

Elihu Root once said, "Politics is the practical exercise of self-government, and somebody must attend to it if we are to have self-government." Making government work is a job for all citizens. It can be a vocation, a calling, or a part-time avocation, but it is worth the serious attention and time of all citizens.

CHAPTER TWELVE

Contact Information
for State Agencies

State agencies on the Internet
http://www.ohio.gov

Adjutant General's Department
2825 West Granville Road
Columbus, Ohio 43235
Telephone (614) 336-6000
http://www.ohionationalguard.com/

Administrative Services, Department of
30 East Broad Street, 40th Floor
Columbus, Ohio 43266-0401
Telephone (614) 466-6511
http://www.das.ohio.gov/

African-American Males, Commission on
35 East Chestnut Street, 5th Floor
Columbus, OH 43215-2541
Telephone (614) 644-5143
Toll Free 1-800-370-4566
http://www.caam.ohio.gov

Aging, Department of
50 West Broad Street, 9th Floor
Columbus, Ohio 43215-3363
Telephone (614) 466-5500
TDD-voice (614) 466-6191
http://www.goldenbuckeye.com

Agriculture, Department of
8995 East Main Street
Reynoldsburg, Ohio 43068
Telephone (614) 728-6200
Toll Free 1-800-282-1955
TDD-Voice 1-800-750-0750
http://www.ohioagriculture.gov

Air Quality Development Authority
50 West Broad Street, Suite 1718
Columbus, Ohio 43215-5985
Telephone (614) 224-3383
http://www.ohioairquality.org

Alcohol and Drug Addiction Services, Department of
280 North High Street, 12th Floor
Columbus, Ohio 43215-2537
Telephone (614) 466-3445
http://www.odadas.state.oh.us

Arts Council, Ohio
727 East Main Street
Columbus, Ohio 43205-1796
Telephone (614) 466-2613
http://www.oac.state.oh.us/

Arts and Sports Facilities Commission
20 East Broad Street, Suite 200
Columbus, Ohio 43215-3416
Telephone (614) 752-2770
http://www.culture.ohio.gov

Athletic Commission, Ohio
Metro Plex
18909 Miles Road
Warrensville Heights, Ohio 44128
Phone: (216) 518-9479
http://aco.ohio.gov/

Attorney General
30 East Broad Street, 17th Floor
Columbus, Ohio 43215-3428
Telephone (614) 466-4320
http://www.ag.state.oh.us

Auditor of State
88 East Broad Street
P.O. Box 1140
Columbus, Ohio 43216-1140
Telephone (614) 466-4514
Toll Free 1-800-282-0370
http://www.auditor.state.oh.us

Budget and Management, Office of
30 East Broad Street, 34th Floor
Columbus, Ohio 43215-3457
Telephone (614) 466-4034
http://www.obm.ohio.gov

Building Authority, Ohio
30 East Broad Street, Suite 4020
Columbus, Ohio 43266-0412
Telephone (614) 466-5959
http://www.oba.ohio.gov

Career Colleges and Schools, State Board of
35 East Gay Street, Suite 403
Columbus, Ohio 43215-3138
Telephone (614) 466-2752
Toll Free 1-877-275-4219
http://www.scr.ohio.gov

Civil Rights Commission, Ohio
1111 East Broad Street, Suite 301
Columbus, Ohio 43205-0543
Telephone (614) 466-2785
Toll free 1-888-278-7101
TTY/TDD (614) 466-9353
http://www.crc.ohio.gov

Commerce, Department of
77 South High Street
Columbus, Ohio 43266-0544
Telephone (614) 466-3636
http://www.com.state.oh.us

Community Service Council, Ohio
51 North High Street, Suite 800
Columbus, Ohio 43215
Telephone (614) 728-2916
http://www.serveohio.org

Consumers' Counsel, Office of
10 West Broad Street
Columbus, Ohio 43215-3485
Telephone (614) 466-8574
Toll Free 1-877-PICK-OCC (742-5622)
http://www.pickocc.org

Correctional Institution Inspection Committee
77 South High Street, 8th Floor
Columbus, Ohio 43215-6108
Telephone (614) 466-6929
http://www.ciic.state.oh.us

Court of Claims of Ohio
65 South Front Street, 3rd Floor
Columbus, Ohio 43215-4131
Telephone (614) 387-9800
http://www.cco.state.oh.us

Criminal Justice Services, Office of
140 East Town Street, Suite 1400
Columbus, Ohio 43215
Phone (614) 466-7782
Toll free 1-888-448-4842
http://www.ocjs.state.oh.us

Development, Department of
77 South High Street, 24th-29th Floors
Columbus, Ohio 43215-6130
Telephone (614) 466-2480
Toll free 1-800-848-1300
http://www.odod.state.oh.us

Dispute Resolution and Conflict Management, Commission on
77 South High Street, 24th Floor
Columbus, Ohio 43266-6108
Telephone (614) 752-9595
http://disputeresolution.ohio.gov

Education, Department of
25 South Front Street
Columbus, Ohio 43215-4183
Telephone (614) 995-1545
Toll Free 1-877-644-6338
http://www.ode.state.oh.us

Education, State Board of
25 S. Front Street, 7th Floor
Columbus, Ohio 43215-4183
Telephone (614)466-5838
Toll Free 1-877-644-6338
http://www.ode.state.oh.us/board

Educational Telecommunications Network Commission of Ohio
2470 North Star Road
Columbus, Ohio 43221-3405
Telephone (614) 644-1714
http://www.oet.edu

Elections Commission, Ohio
21 West Broad Street, Suite 600
Columbus, Ohio 43215-4100
Telephone (614) 466-3205
http://www.elc.ohio.gov

Emergency Management Agency
2855 West Dublin-Granville Road
Columbus, Ohio 43235-2206
Telephone (614) 889-7150
http://www.ema.ohio.gov

Employment Relations Board, State
65 East State Street, 12th Floor
Columbus, Ohio 43215-4213
Telephone (614) 644-8573
http://www.serb.state.oh.us

Environmental Protection Agency, Ohio
122 South Front Street
P.O. Box 1049
Columbus, Ohio 43216-1049
Telephone (614) 644-3020
http://www.epa.state.oh.us

Ethics Commission, Ohio
8 East Long Street, 10th Floor
Columbus, Ohio 43215-2940
Telephone (614) 466-7090
http://www.ethics.ohio.gov/

Governor
77 South High Street
Riffe Center, 30th Floor
Columbus, Ohio 43215-6117
Telephone (614) 466-3555
Governor's Hot Line for Citizen Concerns
(614) 644-HELP
http://www.governor.ohio.gov

Hazardous Waste Facility Board
122 South Front Street
P.O. Box 1049
Columbus, Ohio 43216-1049
Telephone (614) 644-2742
http://www.das.ohio.gov/phone/agency/hws.asp

Health, Department of
246 North High Street
P.O. Box 118
Columbus, Ohio 43266-0118
Telephone (614) 466-3543
http://www.odh.state.oh.us

Highway Patrol, State
P.O. Box 182074
1970 West Broad Street
Columbus, OH 43223-1102
Toll Free 1-877-7PATROL (772-8765)
http://www.statepatrol.ohio.gov

Hispanic/Latino Affairs, Commission on
77 South High Street, 18th Floor
Columbus, Ohio 43266-6108
Telephone (614) 466-8333
http://www.ochla.ohio.gov

Historical Society, Ohio
1982 Velma Avenue
Columbus, Ohio 43211-2453
Telephone (614) 297-2300
http://www.ohiohistory.org

House of Representatives, Ohio
77 South High Street, 10th-14th Floors
Columbus, Ohio 43215-6111
Legislative Information (614) 466-8842
General Information 1-800-282-0253
http://www.house.state.oh.us

Industrial Commission of Ohio
30 West Spring Street
Columbus, Ohio 43215-2233
Telephone (614) 466-6136
Toll free 1-800-521-2691
TDD 1-800-686-1589
http://www.ohioic.com

Inspector General, Office of the
30 East Broad Street, 18th Floor
Columbus, Ohio 43215-3414
Telephone (614) 644-9110
Toll Free Hot Line 1-800-686-1525
http://watchdog.ohio.gov/

Insurance, Department of
2100 Stella Court
Columbus, Ohio 43215-1067
Telephone (614) 644-2658
Consumer Hot Line 1-800-686-1526
http://www.ohioinsurance.gov

Joint Committee on Agency Rule Review
77 South High Street
Columbus, Ohio 43215-6108
Telephone (614) 466-4086
http://www.jcarr.state.oh.us

Lake Erie Commission
One Maritime Place, 4th Floor
Toledo, Ohio 43604-1866
Telephone (419) 245-2514
http://www.epa.state.oh.us/oleo

Legal Rights Services, Ohio
8 East Long Street, 5th Floor
Columbus, Ohio 43215-2999
Telephone (614) 466-7264
TTY (614) 728-2553
Toll free 1-800-282-9181
TTY Toll Free 1-800-858-3542
http://www.olrs.ohio.gov

Legislative Information Office
77 S. High Street, 9th Floor
Columbus, OH 43215
Telephone: (614) 466-2241
Long Distance: 1-800-282-0253

Legislative Inspector General
50 West Broad Street, Suite 1308
Columbus, Ohio 43215-5908
Telephone (614) 728-5100
http://www.jlec-olig.state.oh.us

Legislative Service Commission
77 South High Street, 9th Floor
Columbus, Ohio 43215-6136
Telephone (614) 466-3615
http://www.lsc.state.oh.us

Library of Ohio, State
274 East First Avenue
Columbus, Ohio 43201-3673
Telephone (614) 644-7061
http://winslo.state.oh.us

Lieutenant Governor
77 South High Street, 30th Floor
Columbus, Ohio 43215-0602
Telephone (614) 466-3396
http://www.ltgovernor.ohio.gov/

Liquor Control Commission
77 South High Street, 18th Floor
Columbus, Ohio 43215-6108
Telephone (614) 466-3132
http://www.lcc.ohio.gov/

Lottery Commission, Ohio
615 West Superior Avenue
Cleveland, Ohio 44113-1879
Telephone (216) 787-3200
http://www.ohiolottery.com

Mental Health, Department of
30 East Broad Street, 8th Floor
Columbus, Ohio 43215-3430
Telephone (614) 466-2596
http://www.mh.state.oh.us

Mental Retardation and Developmental Disabilities, Ohio Department of
30 East Broad Street, 12th Floor
Columbus, Ohio 43266-0415
Telephone (614) 466-5214
Toll Free 1-877-464-6733
Hot line for MR/DD Client Abuse Calls 1-866-313-6733
TDD (public info) (614) 466-2999
TDD (consumer affairs) 1-800-228-5405
http://odmrdd.state.oh.us/

Natural Resources, Department of
1930 Belcher Drive
Columbus, Ohio 43224-1387
Telephone (614) 265-6565
http://www.dnr.state.oh.us

Personnel Board of Review
65 East State Street, 12th Floor
Columbus, Ohio 43215-4213
Telephone (614) 466-7046
http://pbr.ohio.gov/

Petroleum Underground Storage Tank Release Compensation Board
50 West Broad Street, Suite 1500
P.O. Box 163188
Columbus, OH 44136-3188
Telephone (614) 752-8963
Toll Free 1-800-224-4659
http://www.petroboard.com/

Public Defender Commission, Ohio
8 East Long Street, 11th Floor
Columbus, Ohio 43266-0587
Telephone (614) 466-5393
Toll free 1-800-686-1573
http://www.opd.ohio.gov

Public Safety, Department of
1970 West Broad Street
P.O. Box 182081
Columbus, Ohio 43223-1102
Telephone (614) 466-2550
http://www.ohiopublicsafety.com

Public Utilities Commission of Ohio
180 East Broad Street
Columbus, Ohio 43215-3793
Telephone (614) 466-3016
TDD - Columbus Area (614) 466-8180
Toll Free 1-800-686-7826
TDD Toll Free 1-800-686-1570
http://www.puco.ohio.gov

Public Works Commission
65 East State Street, Suite 312
Columbus, Ohio 43215-4213
Telephone (614) 466-0880
http://www.pwc.state.oh.us

Board of Regents, Ohio
30 East Broad Street, 36th Floor
Columbus, Ohio 43215-3413
Telephone (614) 466-6000
http://www.regents.state.oh.us

Rehabilitation and Correction, Department of
1050 Freeway Drive North
Columbus, Ohio 43229-5490
Telephone (614) 752-1159
http://www.drc.state.oh.us

Rehabilitation Services Commission
400 East Campus View Boulevard
Columbus, Ohio 43235-4604
Telephone (Voice & TDD) (614) 438-1200
Toll Free (Voice & TDD) 1-800-282-4636
http://www.rsc.ohio.gov

Retirement Study Council, Ohio
88 East Broad Street, Suite 1175
Columbus, Ohio 43215-3525
Telephone (614) 228-1346
http://www.orsc.org

RETIREMENT SYSTEMS
Ohio State Highway Patrol Retirement System
6161 Busch Boulevard, Suite 119
Columbus, Ohio 43229-2508
Telephone (614) 431-0781
Toll Free 1-800-860-2268
http://www.ohprs.org

Ohio Police and Fire Pension Fund
140 East Town Street
Columbus, Ohio 43215
Telephone (614) 228-2975
TTY (614) 221-3846
Retirement and Survivors 1-800-860-9599
Active Members 1-888-864-8363
http://www.pfdpf.org/

Ohio Public Employees Retirement System
277 East Town Street
Columbus, Ohio 43215-4642
Telephone (614) 466-2085
Toll Free 1-800-222-PERS *(7377)*
http://www.opers.org/

School Employees Retirement System of Ohio
300 E. Broad Street, Suite 100
Columbus, OH 43215-3746
Columbus area: (614) 222-5853
Members toll-free: (866) 280-7377
Retirees toll-free: (800) 878-5853
http://www.ohsers.org

State Teachers Retirement System of Ohio
275 East Broad Street
Columbus, OH 43215-3771
Telephone (614) 227-4090
Toll Free 1-888-227-7877
http://www.strsoh.org

Rural Development Partnership
8995 East Main Street
Reynoldsburg, Ohio 43068-3399
Telephone (614) 720-4937
http://www.ohioagriculture.gov/ordp.stm

Secretary of State
30 East Broad Street, 16th Floor
Columbus, Ohio 43215-3414
Telephone (614) 466-2655
Toll free 1-877-767-6446
http://www.sos.state.oh.us

Senate, Ohio
The Statehouse
Columbus, Ohio 43215-4147
Legislative Information (614) 466-4900
General Information 1-800-282-0253
http://www.senate.state.oh.us

Supreme Court of Ohio
65 South Front Street
Columbus, Ohio 43215-3431
Telephone (614) 387-9000
Toll Free 1-800-826-9010
http://www.sconet.state.oh.us

Tax Appeals, Board of
30 East Broad Street, 24th Floor
Columbus, Ohio 43215-3414
Telephone (614) 466-6700
http://www.bta.ohio.gov

Taxation, Department of
30 East Broad Street, 22nd Floor
Columbus, Ohio 43266-0420
Telephone (614) 466-5234
Individual Income Taxpayer Services 1-800-282-1780
Individual Refund Hot Line 1-800-282-1784
http://www.tax.ohio.gov

Transportation, Department of
1980 West Broad Street
Columbus, OH 43223-1102
Telephone (614) 466-7170
http://www.dot.state.oh.us/

Treasurer of State
30 East Broad Street, 9th Floor
Columbus, Ohio 43266-0421
Telephone (614) 466-2160
TTY 1-800-228-1102
http://www.treasurer.state.oh.us

Water Development Authority
480 South High Street
Columbus, Ohio 43215-5603
Telephone (614) 466-5822
Toll Free 1-877-OWDA-123 *(6932)*
http://www.owda.org/

Workers' Compensation, Bureau of
30 West Spring Street
Columbus, Ohio 43215-2241
Telephone (614) 466-6292
Toll Free 1-800-OHIO-BWC *(644-6292)*
TDD 1-800-BWC-4-TDD *(292-4833)*
http://www.ohiobwc.com

Youth Services, Department of
51 North High Street
Columbus, Ohio 43215-3098
Telephone (614) 466-4314
http://www.dys.ohio.gov

Selected Bibliography

Goodman, Rebecca. "State admitted to Union 150 years later." *Cincinnati Enquirer*, 7 Aug. 2003.

Legislative Service Commission. *A Guidebook for Ohio Legislators*. Columbus, OH, 2003.

Legislative Service Commission. *Members Only*, Vol. 124, Issue 5. Columbus, OH, 12 Feb. 2001.

Ohio Courts Futures Commission. *Final Report: A Changing Landscape*. Columbus, OH, 2000.

Ohio Criminal Sentencing Commission. *A Plan for Felony Sentencing in Ohio*. Columbus, OH, 2002.

Ohio Criminal Sentencing Commission. *A Plan for Misdemeanor Sentencing in Ohio*. Columbus, OH, 2002.

Ohio Municipal League. *Municipal Government in Ohio*. Columbus, OH, 2004.

Ohio Office of Budget and Management. *The Ohio Budgetary Financial Report*. Columbus, OH, 2003.

Ohio Revised Code, http://www.onlinedocs.andersonpublishing.com

Secretary of State. "A Guide to Candidate Requirements in the 2004 Elections." Columbus, OH, 2004.

Secretary of State. Constitution of the State of Ohio. Columbus, OH, 1999.

Secretary of State. *Ohio Voter Information Guide: A citizen's outline of Ohio's 2004 elections, registration and voting process*. Columbus, OH, 2004.

State of Ohio Government Agencies, http://www.ohio.gov

Supreme Court of Ohio. "The Supreme Court of Ohio." Columbus, OH, 2004.

U.S. Department of Commerce, Census Bureau. *2002 Census of Governments*, Vol. 1, Number 1, Government Organization, GC02(1)-1. U.S. Government Printing Office. Washington, D.C., 2002.

Index

For more information about
the League of Women Voters of Ohio,
to submit comments about this publication,
and to order this or other League publications,
visit our Web site at **http://www.lwvohio.org**,
e-mail **sales@lwvohio.org**,
or call **(614) 469-1505**.